What People Are Saying about *Gluten-Free 101*...

"Carol Fenster's infectious enthusiasm for gluten free cooking totally captivated me at the national meeting of the American Dietetic Association. Her recipes in Gluten-Free 101 *make gluten free cooking delicious, quick and fun! I recommend her books to all my patients but don't reserve her good dishes only for those on a gluten free diet—they're too good not to share."*—**Cynthia S. Rudert, MD, FACP, Medical Advisor, Celiac Disease Foundation; Medical Advisor, Gluten Intolerance Group; Private Practice Gastroenterology, Atlanta, Georgia**

"Carol is known as the 'gluten-free goddess' because she creates the best French bread, mouth-watering pie crusts, delectable desserts, and a phenomenal pizza. You must get this book.—**Shelley Case, BSc, RD, author of Gluten-Free Diet: A Comprehensive Resource Guide**

"If you are not a cook, cooking gluten-free can be difficult, at best. In Gluten-Free 101, *Carol Fenster has given you all the information you need to get started and be successful. A wonderful flour blend used in many of the easy recipes, tips on stocking your pantry and the equipment needed. Using this book, you can be a successful gluten-free cook your first time in the kitchen."*—**Cynthia Kupper, RD, CD, Executive Director, Gluten Intolerance Group of North America**.

"Eating gluten free means you have to dust off your cooking and baking skills. This book will help you feel confident and in control of your gluten-free kitchen."—**Ann Whelan, publisher of *Gluten-Free Living***

*"*Gluten-Free 101 *serves up a feast of easy, classic recipes with a bonus new versatile flour mix (with more nutrients and fiber) that can be tailored to individual tastes. Carol's experience in cooking and writing wheat-free, gluten-free cookbooks helps the "newbie" or "old-timer" be successful in creating basic recipes.*—**Janet Y. Rinehart, Former President of CSA/USA; President, Houston Celiac Support Group**

*"*Gluten-Free 101 *is an excellent resource for anyone learning to live gluten free. Carol Fenster has done a superb job of putting together some great recipes with the detailed information needed to prepare them."*—**Mary K. Sharrett, MS, RD, LD, CNSD, Children's Hospital, Columbus, OH**

"Carol's Gluten-Free 101 *is the most descriptive, informative book I have seen yet. But Carol goes a step further by adding personal example that demonstrates her passion for gluten-free living!"*—**Shannon T. Bishop, RD, Clinical Dietitian, HealthONE Presbyterian/St. Luke's Medical Center; Director of Nutrition & Wellness, Transformations, Inc.; and National Talk-show Host, VoiceAmerica**

"Another success! Carol's talent for simplifying is the best in the business. If you only have time to read one book on gluten-free cooking, THIS is the book."—**Betsy Prohaska Hicks, Diet Counselor and Author of "Cooking Healthy Gluten and Casein-Free Food for Children"**

"Excellent! This is book is just what my patients need to answer their questions and empower them towards healing. Carol has the talent of taking basic knowledge and transforming it into concise and powerful information that is easy to read and reference. The visual charts are outstanding, and her recipes never fail to delight her readers."—**John H. Hicks, MD, FAAP, Pathways Medical Advocates**

GLUTEN-FREE 101
EASY, BASIC DISHES WITHOUT WHEAT

Carol Fenster, Ph.D.

Savory Palate, Inc.
8174 South Holly, # 404
Centennial, CO 80122-4004
www.GlutenFree101.com

Printed in the United States of America
First Printing, 2003
2nd Printing, 2004
3rd Printing, 2005
4th Printing, 2006
5th Printing, 2008
Although the author and publisher have exhaustively researched many sources to ensure the accuracy and completeness of the information in this book, we assume no responsibility for errors, inaccuracies, omissions, or any inconsistency herein. No information contained herein should be construed as medical advice or as a guarantee that individuals will tolerate foods prepared from these recipes.

Library of Congress Catalog Card Number 2002096495

ISBN-13: 1-978-1889374-08-6
ISBN-10: 1-889374-08-3

Gluten-Free 101: Easy, Basic Dishes without Wheat by Carol Fenster, PhD

SUMMARY
1. Gluten-free cookbook, gluten-free diet, gluten-free food, wheat-free diet
2. Wheat intolerance, gluten intolerance, wheat sensitivity, wheat allergy, food allergy, asthma, autism, gluten sensitive enteropathy, dermatitis herpetiformis

Edited by Mary Bonner; Helke Farin, MD
Cover by Karen Saunders of MacGraphics Services, Aurora, CO
Artwork by Helke Farin, MD

For more information, contact:
Savory Palate, Inc., 8174 South Holly, #404, Centennial, CO 80122-4004.
Visit www.glutenfree101.com

To my grandchildren Keene, Romi, and Cole. I love you.

☞ Acknowledgements ☜

I have many people to thank for their help with this book. A special thanks to my testers: Anne Barfield, Jamie & Lisa Bridges, Julie Cary, Caroline Herdle, Debbie Lee, Chrissy Rowland, Judy Sarver, Chris Silker, Leen Spear, Anne Washburn, Betty Wass, Cecile Weed, and Sue Weilgopolan—and to their families and friends for lending their critical palates to the tasting process. I truly appreciate your contribution!

I am also deeply indebted to the following professionals who gave me their wonderfully informative, constructive feedback: Shannon T. Bishop, RD, Presbyterian/St. Luke's Medical Center, Denver, CO; Mary Bonner; Shelley Case, BSc, RD, Case Nutrition Consulting; Helke Farin, MD; John H. Hicks, MD, Pathways Medical Advocates; Cynthia Kupper, RD, Executive Director, Gluten Intolerance Group of North America; Betsy Prohaska Hicks, Pathways Medical Advocates; Janet Rinehart, Past-president of CSA/USA, Inc. and current president, Houston Celiac Sprue Association; Peggy Wagener, Publisher, *Living Without* magazine; and Ann Whelan, Publisher, *Gluten-Free Living* magazine

And, finally—thanks to my wonderful family, especially my husband Larry for his patience, support, and encouragement.

෬• Contents •ෂ

Other books by Carol Fenster, Ph.D.
or from Savory Palate, Inc.

1,000 Gluten-Free Recipes (John C. Wiley & Sons, 2008)
by Carol Fenster

Gluten-Free Quick & Easy—From Prep to Plate without the Fuss:
200+ Recipes for People with Food Sensitivities (Avery/Penguin Group, 2007)
by Carol Fenster, Ph.D.

Cooking Free:
200 Flavorful Recipes for People with Food Allergies
and Multiple Food Sensitivities (Avery/Penguin Group, 2005)
By Carol Fenster, PhD

Wheat-Free Recipes & Menus:
Delicious, Healthful Eating for People with Food Sensitivities, (Avery/Penguin Group, 2004)
By Carol Fenster, PhD

Food Allergy Field Guide:
A Lifestyle Manual for Families (Savory Palate, 2006)
By Theresa Willingham

Gluten-Free Friends: An Activity Book for Kids (Savory Palate, 2003)
By Nancy Patin Falini, MA, RD, LDN

♥• Preface •♥

If you have read my previous cookbooks such as *Wheat-Free Recipes & Menus* or *Cooking Free or Gluten-Free Quick & Easy,* you know that I did not intend to become a cookbook author. Writing cookbooks—especially gluten-free cookbooks—was not part of my life plan. But, life is full of ironies, isn't it?

You see, I'm the daughter of a Nebraska farmer—a farmer who raised wheat. Wheat was a good thing at our house. It put food on the table and paid for my college tuition. After college, I married into a wheat-farming family. In fact, that's all they raise on their farm in western Nebraska. Furthermore, my father-in-law is an internationally-known Professor Emeritus of Agronomy at the University of Nebraska. What is his main area of expertise? You guessed it—wheat!

At first, after I discovered my sensitivity to the gluten protein in wheat, I thought I was the only person in the world who had to avoid this seemingly healthy food. At least I certainly didn't know anyone else with this life-altering situation and back in 1988, there wasn't much information on the topic. The Internet, as we know it today, didn't exist. I was in a state of denial for some time, bewildered by this unexpected turn of events that disrupted my otherwise wonderful life. There were virtually no gluten-free foods on the market, so I revamped my entire repertoire of dishes. Over time, I met more and more people who also avoided wheat and realized that my new recipes could help others. The idea for a cookbook was born.

Gluten-Free—New Diet for the 21st Century
Twenty years later, I know that I'm one of several million people with a gluten-free lifestyle. My books are purchased all over the world because the gluten-free lifestyle isn't confined to the U.S. I help companies develop gluten-free products and my gluten-free culinary skills are applied internationally (e.g., in Japan, where wheat is a major allergen). Compared to 1988, when I couldn't find anything to eat we now have a wonderful array of ready-made foods, mixes, and ingredients. Our gluten-free meals rival any served in restaurants or featured in magazines.

When I started my publishing and consulting business in 1995, many other things were happening as well. As I said, the gluten-free diet was considered unusual. Celiac disease was virtually unknown to the general public. The medical community didn't pay much attention to celiac disease, calling it a "rare" condition. Mainstream manufacturers, restaurants, and other businesses in the food industry barely acknowledged the gluten-free diet, leaving the field wide open for a handful of specialized entrepreneurs like me who tried to fill the void with cookbooks, mixes, and a few ready-made foods. Specialized magazines appeared such as *Gluten-Free Living* and *Living Without*. My cookbooks were eventually joined by others, giving us more choices when we cook at home.

Today, the gluten-free diet is IN! Leading universities such as Columbia, Harvard, and Stanford as well as the Universities of Chicago, Maryland, and San Diego—and the Mayo Clinic in Rochester, MN—have established celiac research centers. Restaurants offer gluten-free dishes, new gluten-free foods appear on grocery shelves or are available from an extensive array of on-line vendors, and the gluten-free diet is mentioned frequently in mainstream magazines.

In 2003, leaders in the gluten-free community formed the American Celiac Task Force to present a unified voice to government, the food industry, and the public on food labeling. That group is now known as the American Celiac Disease Alliance and its efforts, along with many dedicated leaders and elected officials, resulted in the Food Allergen Labeling and Consumer Protection Act (FALCPA). Beginning January, 2006, food manufactured in the U.S. must state the eight major food allergens, including wheat, on the food label in plain English.

In 2004, the National Institutes of Health (NIH) Celiac Consensus Conference defined celiac disease, its diagnosis, treatment, and prevalence. According to the University of Chicago Celiac Disease Center web site, celiac disease affects more people than those with Parkinson's disease (1,000,000), or Rheumatoid Arthritis (2.1 million), or Lupus (1.5 million) or Multiple sclerosis (400,000). With celiac disease, however, there is no pill, no vaccine, and no surgical procedure. The only treatment is a gluten-free diet for life.

As I write this, we await the Food and Drug Administration (FDA) ruling on the definition of the term "gluten-free." (See www.gluten.net, www.celiac.org, or www.glutenfreediet.ca for an update on this ruling.) I hope that reading these last few paragraphs has filled you with hope that our diet is becoming increasingly accepted as a viable lifestyle, not just a fad or fashionable trend. And, it's only going to get better. If there was ever a time to be gluten-free, it's now.

—Carol Fenster, Ph.D

☜• Introduction •☞

T he year was 1988. I finally knew the cause for my lifetime bout with chronic sinusitis. My physician had absolutely *delighted* me with his diagnosis. All I had to do was avoid gluten and I would be cured. No more sinus headaches, no more antibiotics, and no more laryngitis.

Unfortunately, my euphoria lasted until that evening's meal. As I contemplated my choices for dinner that night, I realized that this wasn't going to be so easy after all. To make matters worse, I am one of those people who "live to eat" rather than "eat to live." Food is my passion, my comfort, my joy. I had to find a way to continue eating my favorites—bagels, fresh-baked bread, cakes, brownies—without gluten.

Thus began the journey of discourse, dishes, and discovery that culminates in this—my 4th—book on the topic of gluten-free living. But I've learned a lot on this journey. I'm writing this book so you can quickly grasp and easily apply the essentials of a gluten-free diet to your everyday life.

Where to Get Help
Fortunately, there are many organizations that provide more detailed information about food sensitivities. You'll find them listed in the Appendix, under Associations. Some focus on food allergies, some on celiac disease, while others focus on autism. You should contact them, visit their web sites, and submit your annual dues to support their work and receive their informative newsletters. Attend their annual conferences and make new friends who live the same way as you. Check the Appendix for selected books and web sites on food sensitivities.

My View on Special Diets
I never refer to the gluten-free diet as a restricted, limited, or alternative diet. Instead, I refer to it as part of a "special" diet because it is tailored to suit the needs of those who can't eat gluten. I'm very aware of the psychological aspects of adjusting to this way of eating in terms of the grief, denial, and anger that accompany loss of any kind—especially your favorite foods.

However, it is very important to refer to your diet with a positive, rather than negative outlook. Our bodies hear what our brains are thinking, so keep your thoughts and actions positive at all times. To me, "special" is a positive term. Whenever I'm tempted by forbidden food, I remind myself that "Nothing tastes as good as feeling good feels." I then imagine how I will feel if I eat the forbidden food and that's enough to make me realize it isn't worth it.

A Quick Overview of This Book

Here is a quick overview of this book to help you eat well without gluten:

Introduction: Getting started with a quick list of prepared foods to eat right now!

Gluten: A Real Pain in the Gut: Why you can't have gluten. Where to get help. Living without—gluten psychologically and emotionally.

Going Against the Grain: Gluten-free flours for baking.

The Name Game: Where gluten can and can't be found. Reading labels.

Get Going—Gluten-Free: Travel and dine away from home safely.

Gluten-Free Kitchen: How to make one easy, versatile flour blend for everything. Setting up a gluten-free kitchen. Choosing helpful appliances like bread machines plus secrets to their success. Comprehending mysterious culinary terms.

Recipes: Recipes for breads, breakfast, desserts, main dishes.

Getting Started

For most people, learning what's wrong is actually quite liberating. At least we know who the enemy is. However, I recall walking into my kitchen for the first time after my diagnosis and realizing just how many of my old favorites were off-limits! There was food in the kitchen, yet the cupboards were locked.

Well, here are a few foods you can safely eat and readily find at your grocery store or natural food store. Of course, always read labels on everything. Companies alter their manufacturing practices and ingredients so labels can change. As time goes on, you will naturally add to your list of acceptable foods. You don't want to be like my friend who avoided breakfast for three months because she couldn't figure out what to eat.

ℭℬ• Gluten-Free Starter Guide •℘

Breakfast

Cold Cereal	Hot Cereal
Brown Rice Crisps (Erewhon)	Amaranth Flakes (NuWorldAmaranth)
Crispy Brown Rice, Aztec (Erewhon, Kinnikinnick)	Millet Grits (Bob's Red Mill)
Corn Flakes (Erewhon)	Cream of Buckwheat (Birkett Mills)
EnviroKids Cereals (Nature's Path)	Cream of Rice (Erewhon)
Granola (Bakery on Main, Enjoy Life)	Hot & Creamy (Lundberg)
Nutty Rice/Nutty Flax Cereal (Enjoy Life)	Mighty Fine Cereal (Bob's Red Mill)
Maple Buckwheat (Arrowhead Mills)	Oatmeal (Bob's Red Mill, Cream Hill Estates, Gifts of Nature, Gluten-Free Oats, Only Oats)
Puffed Amaranth (NuWorldAmaranth)	Quinoa Flakes (Ancient Harvest, Altiplano)

Eggs, bacon, ham, fruit, hash browns—if prepared without gluten in sauces, dusting, flavoring, or handling. Sausage *may* contain wheat fillers.

Lunch

Cold	Hot
Lettuce Salads (gf salad dressings only)	Soup* (bean, tomato, Manhattan clam chowder, split pea, chili)
Sandwiches (Food for Life or Whole Foods bread)	Enchiladas (with corn tortillas or tortilla wraps from Food for Life)
Wraps (Food for Life or LaTortilla Factory)	*unless thickened with wheat flour*
Deli cold cuts (Boar's Head)	
Pasta Salad (pasta by Dr. Shar, Ener-G, Pastariso, De-Boles, Annie Chun's, Heartland, Tinkyada)	

Dinner

Main Dishes	Desserts	
Roasted/Baked/Grilled Meats (Beef, Pork, Chicken, or Fish)	Fresh Fruit	Pudding/Custard*
Spaghetti Sauce on Pasta (Dr. Shar, Ener-G, Annie, Pastariso, DeBolles, Heartland's Finest, Tinkyada)	Baked Apples	Cookies (Pamela's or Enjoy Life)
	Ice cream*	Macaroons*
Side Dishes	Sorbet	Meringue Cups
Baked Potatoes....Brown Rice...Whole Grains	Flourless Cakes	
Steamed/Roasted/Grilled Veggies	*unless prepared with wheat flour*	

Snacks

Rice bran crackers (Health Valley)	Pretzels (Ener-G, Glutino)
Cookies (Pamela's or Enjoy Life or Ener-G)	Raisins & other dried fruit
Crackers (HolGrain, San J, Blue Diamond, Lundberg, Edward&Sons, Mary's Gone Crackers, Ener-G)	Fresh fruits and vegetables
Fruit leather Nuts	Popcorn Plain corn chips
Hummus Bars (Lara)	

Meal Planning

Starting September, 2008, I offer a gluten-free weekly online menu planning service to help you in meal planning. See www.gfreecuisine.com for more information.

Fiber Is Your Friend

For years our focus has been on the *safety* of gluten-free food. Is it *really* gluten-free? The flours we originally used were primarily the highly refined white or brown rice flours. We then mixed them with other highly refined starches such as potato, corn, or tapioca. Without other sources of fiber, the results are baked items that are high in refined carbohydrates and low in protein and fiber.

The American Dietetic Association recommends 25 to 38 grams of fiber per day, yet the average American only gets 12 to 17 grams daily (Digestive Health & Nutrition, Nov/Dec 2002). Fortunately, there are many new flours with higher protein and fiber contents—such as bean, sorghum, amaranth, Montina (Indian ricegrass), quinoa—and flours made from nuts. The mixes I recommend in this book feature some of these flours.

With all the emphasis on fiber today, you should give some thought to other ways of increasing your fiber intake. Eating lots of fresh fruit and vegetables will help (especially with the skins on), as well as substituting whole grains such as cooked brown rice for low-fiber cereals like cream of rice. Nuts and flax meal are terrific sources of fiber; toss some on your cereal or yogurt. Beans are an excellent source of nutrients and important fiber. Add whole cannellini beans or chickpeas to salads, eat bean soups, or mash whole white beans into hummus.

In baking, add a couple tablespoons of rice bran or flaxseed meal or quinoa flakes to the bread or muffin dough. Gradually increase that amount to ¼ to ⅓ cup per recipe. Rice Innovations—makers of Pastariso and Pastato pasta—developed a new, high-fiber spaghetti to meet this need. Look for it at your health food store.

Nutrient Content of Recipes

All recipes are nutritionally analyzed with Food Processor software by ESHA Research or nutrient analysis software by MasterCook Deluxe. Nutrient data includes: calories, fat, protein, carbohydrates, sodium, cholesterol, and fiber. Serving size is defined by the American Dietetic Association. When ingredient choices are listed, the analysis is for the first choice. All analyses use the Flour Blend containing corn flour (page 41) and 2% milk. I've made every effort to make these recipes as healthy as possible, without sacrificing taste or texture.

✁• Gluten: A Real Pain in the Gut •✂

Unless you're a baker or a food scientist, most of us go through life not knowing or caring much about gluten. That's why our gluten sensitivity comes as such a surprise. We didn't know gluten existed in the first place!

Nonetheless, gluten (a protein in wheat and related grains such as barley, rye, spelt, kamut, and triticale) plays a major role in many medical conditions. I'll give you a brief explanation of these conditions and point you toward resources that provide more details. I urge you to follow through and check out these resources so that you can get the full picture instead of just the snapshot I provide here.

Wheat Allergies and Intolerances
Wheat is one of the top eight food allergens. We don't know which of the proteins in wheat is the actual culprit for those with intolerances or allergies to it, but we do know that people can be deathly allergic to wheat.

I know of one young man so desperately allergic to wheat that if he inhales the tiny particles of flour that waft through the kitchen during baking, he experiences an anaphylactic reaction and must be treated with an epinephrine injection to "buy" him enough time to get to an emergency room. The IgE antibodies in his system react to the wheat and this reaction can be fatal.

For other people, wheat is bothersome, but not necessarily life-threatening. Like me, they have a wheat intolerance. This means that the IgG antibodies in our systems react to wheat, although different people may experience different types of reactions.

My response to wheat is nasal congestion and stuffiness, often resulting in sinus infections. Other people have stomach aches, headaches, rashes, joint aches, fatigue, or brain fog—to name just a few symptoms. Wheat may not kill those of us with wheat intolerances, but it certainly compromises the quality of our lives.

True allergies must be diagnosed by an allergist but some allergists don't believe in intolerances and may not perform these tests.

Celiac Disease (Celiac Sprue)

Less well known but perhaps far more prevalent—once called the "common disease no one's heard of"—is celiac disease (also called celiac sprue, or related forms of gluten intolerance or gluten sensitive enteropathy or GSE).

> *"Celiac—the common disease no one's heard of."*

It is a genetically transmitted condition in which gluten (a protein in wheat and related grains) damages the small intestine's ability to absorb food nutrients. Another form of GSE—dermatitis herpetiformis (DH)— causes skin rashes and blister-like spots.

According to the Center for Celiac Research at the University of Maryland, approximately 1 in 133 people in the United States have celiac disease. Other parts of the world such as Great Britain, Ireland, and Northern Europe report a 1 in 300 incidence in the general population. It is no longer an uncommon disease.

Persons with celiac disease must avoid all forms of gluten, found in wheat and wheat-related grains such as barley, rye, and spelt, as well as the lesser-known grains of kamut and triticale. Regular oats—which do not inherently contain gluten—may be contaminated with wheat during the growing and manufacturing process and remain off-limits. Pure, uncontaminated gluten-free oats are now available in natural food stores and at www.bobsredmill.com, www.creamhillestates.com, www.giftsofnature.net, and www.glutenfreeoats.com, and www.onlyoats.com). Check with your physician about eating these oats.

Celiac disease is a lifelong condition requiring strict adherence to a gluten-free diet. The condition is diagnosed by a gastroenterologist; then dietitians help patients manage the new diet. See the Appendix for national associations with celiac information.

Where Can I Find Help?

There are many different approaches to living with food sensitivities. My advice is to read as much as possible about the physical consequences of food sensitivities—but also about the psychological, sociological, and emotional issues that we all face when the doctor says "no more gluten". Two books that will help are *Celiac Disease: a Hidden Epidemic* by Peter H.R. Green and Rory Jones and *Recognizing Celiac Disease – The Complete Guide to Recognizing, Diagnosing & Managing Celiac Disease by* Cleo J. Libonati. A video by Michelle Pietzak, MD, *"Gluten Free MD: Symptoms, Diagnosis, and Treatment of Celiac Disease and*

Gluten Intolerance is also very helpful. An excellent book that will help you understand the nutritional aspects of the celiac diet is *Gluten-Free Diet: A Comprehensive Resource Guide, Expanded Edition* by Shelley Case, BSc, RD. If your children have celiac disease or other food sensitivities, you will find help in *Food Allergy Field Guide: a Lifestyle Manual for Families* by Theresa Willingham and *Kids with Celiac Disease: A Family Guide to Raising Happy, Healthy Gluten-Free Children* by Danna Korn. Danna founded a national support group network called R.O.C.K. (Raising Our Celiac Kids) at www.celiackids.com.

Other books that will enlighten you about celiac disease, gluten allergies and intolerances, and other gluten-sensitive conditions include *Dangerous Grains: Why Gluten Cereal Grains May Be Hazardous to Your Health* by James Braly, MD, and Ron Hoggan, MA; *Food Allergy Relief* by James Braly, MD, et al.; and *Dr. Braly's Food Allergy and Nutrition Revolution: For Permanent Weight Loss and a Longer, Healthier Life* by James Braly, MD and Laura Torbet.

Two excellent magazines that are very helpful to people with gluten sensitivities are *Living Without* and *Gluten-Free Living*. (See Appendix.) Another good resource is *Scott-Free*, a newsletter from the founder of the Gluten-Free Mall. The newsletters of the national associations are also extremely helpful. (See Appendix.)

For information on how gluten is related to autism and other developmental disorders see *Special Diets for Special Kids* by Lisa Lewis, Ph.D., and *Unraveling the Mystery of Autism and Pervasive Developmental Disorder: A Mother's Story of Research and Recovery* by Karyn Seroussi and Bernard Rimland, PhD, and *Louder Than Words* by Jenny McCarthy. Betsy Prohaska Hick's videos are excellent: "Cooking Healthy Gluten and Casein-Free Food for Children" and "The Comprehensive GFCD Diet Video". You may order them at www.gfcf.com. This web site is also a good source for learning more about the gluten-free, casein-free diet for autism.

This book is meant as a beginner's guide to provide you with the basics. You might like to move on to my other cookbooks (see them at my web site at www.glutenfree101.com) or examine other gluten-free cookbooks to find ones best suited to your way of eating. There are many ways to live gluten-free and my style of dining is just one of many ways to approach the gluten-free lifestyle.

There are now several major celiac research centers at leading universities across the nation. These centers hold major conferences and the faculty at each of them publish important research on the gluten-free condition. See the Appendix for a list of those universities and centers. Each had an excellent web site to provide further information as well.

Living with Food Sensitivities

Being diagnosed with a food sensitivity is like any other loss involving the stages of denial, anger and, finally, acceptance. I went through all these stages. Here's how I adopted a new lifestyle:

First, get a reliable diagnosis. This is important so you know *exactly* what you *can* and *can't* eat. All too often, patients try to diagnose themselves and end up confused, frustrated, and unsure of what's really bothering them. Furthermore, they might unnecessarily omit very nutritious foods from their diets without adequate replacements.

"The average celiac takes between 4 and 10 years to get a diagnosis."

If your symptoms are gastrointestinal (e.g., bloating, diarrhea, constipation, or gas), a gastroenterologist should test you for celiac disease. Often, patients correctly suspect food as the culprit, but *incorrectly* assume that they should see an allergist. But an allergist only tests for allergies. Celiac disease is *not* an allergy so the test results are often negative. This leaves the patients believing that food isn't the problem and so they resume eating the *very* foods they should actually avoid.

To further complicate matters, only about one-third of people with celiac disease actually experience the "typical" symptoms (e.g., diarrhea) outlined in the paragraph above. Others may just experience fatigue; still others may have no symptoms at all. Some people "accidentally" learn that they have celiac disease when other problems such as anemia or osteoporosis become evident.

According to the experts, the average celiac takes between 4 and 10 years to get a diagnosis (www.celiacdisease.net and *Celiac Disease: A Hidden Epidemic* by Peter Green, M.D., and Rory Jones). In the meantime, many go from doctor to doctor searching for answers.

Many such patients come to believe that they suffer from some other unknown malady, *or* they're told "it's all in your head", *or* they're accused of using a food sensitivity to "get attention." I personally heard these very things from well-meaning physicians. They are no longer my physicians.

I'm not a celiac nor am I allergic to wheat. I have a wheat intolerance—I don't digest wheat well. When tested for true allergies, my results are negative because these tests search for IgE antibodies, rather than the IgG antibodies characteristic of wheat intolerances. However, I eat the same diet as those with celiac disease.

Vent your feelings. Honor your feelings by expressing them. Join a support group, share your thoughts, and listen to the feelings of others. It will help you put your situation in perspective and allow you to let off steam in the process.

In addition, support groups provide valuable information on how to manage a gluten-free diet—including recipes as well as tips on cooking, shopping, reading labels, and eating out. See the Appendix for associations. (CDF, CSA/USA, or GIG may have a group in your city.)

If you have a close friend or family member who's willing to listen without judging, share your thoughts with them. Get their input. Ask them to support your efforts to avoid gluten. People who are with you every day need to *"Family members may sabotage our diets."* understand *why* you can't eat your particular food culprit and where it might be lurking.

Enlist family, friends, and co-workers to form your own private support group. This is very important because family members unwittingly (or sometimes knowingly) sabotage our diet efforts (just like husbands who give chocolates to their dieting wives).

And, don't forget that family members may initially regard your food sensitivity as a threat to *their* way of life. They don't want to give up *their* favorite foods just because *you* can't have them. Be open and honest with them about your needs. Ask for their help.

Learn to prepare or choose foods that don't compromise meal time at your house. At my house, we eat gluten-free because that's the only choice I provide. My family and my guests enjoy all the usual foods, except I serve them in gluten-free versions.

Accept the facts and get on with your life. You can no longer eat with abandon; you have to examine every morsel of food. Your world seems like it's tilting out of control because you think you can't have the customary birthday cake…or join your friends for coffee and pastry at your favorite coffee house…or simply eat pizza.

It's OK to have feelings of anger or even guilt. You may even try to blame that ancestor who passed on the celiac genes to you *or* your parents from whom you inherited your food allergies. (If you're born into a family with allergies, your chance of having allergies is 50 to 60% higher. Talk about "lucky" genes!)

Well, get over it! Accept the facts and be grateful that all you have to do is control what you eat. That's a lot better than having a terminal illness or losing a limb or being horribly ill every day of your life. Choose to look at your cup as half-full, not half-empty. Back to that pizza…did you know there are several gluten-free beers to eat with your gluten-free pizza? This is great news for beer lovers and proof that our gluten-free lifestyle is improving.

It's also important to accept the fact that you can't have even a little bit of the forbidden food. It took me five years to learn this. With my demanding executive lifestyle and constant travel, I thought I could eat a little bit of wheat now and then. Wrong!

But eventually—after all the anger, tears, denial, and guilt—most of us accept the hard, cold facts that we can't eat certain foods. That's when we're ready to learn about alternative ways of dining.

Don't whine, complain, or express sorrow for yourself. Most people live with some sort of inability or disability. Dwelling on it makes you a bore. Learn to answer questions about your condition with tact. If you don't want to go into the gory details, simply answer, "Wheat makes me feel sick." Or, "wheat doesn't agree with me so I don't eat it." Or, simply say, "No thanks."

Learn to cook or—if you don't want to cook—at least know how to choose prepared foods wisely. In the end, you're responsible for what you eat. When you cook in your own kitchen, you have control over what goes into your food and the standards under which it is prepared.

Even though my husband and I love to dine out, we always know the best (and safest) food is served in my own kitchen. Even though manufacturers are producing more gluten-free foods and restaurants are becoming more knowledgeable, you'll fare better if you develop some basic cooking skills. The better you get at cooking, the more your food will look and taste like the "real thing."

Make small changes first. Of course, you have to give up gluten entirely. But rather than trying to learn how to cook (or buy) everything in one week, master a basic recipe first and adapt it to your way of life. For example, my Basic Muffin recipe can be made into a variety of different flavors, as can the Basic Bread.

Allow time for your palate to adjust. We Americans expect baked goods to taste like wheat because we've grown accustomed to the taste. Celiacs who once learned to like bread made from rice flour now find that it takes time to adjust to the newer flours made from beans, sorghum, or quinoa.

Read labels. The Food Allergen Labeling and Consumer Protection Act (FALCPA) that took effect on January 1, 2006, makes it easier to determine the safety of food by reading the label. Each of the top eight allergens (wheat, milk, eggs, soy, peanuts, tree nuts, fish, and shellfish) must be clearly stated—in plain English—on the label if they are among the ingredients. While this law doesn't cover other gluten-containing foods such as barley, rye, or spelt, these items will be included in the ingredient label so you'll know if gluten is present.

Purchase the guides published by the Celiac Sprue Association/USA, Tri-County Celiac Support Group, or Clan Thompson (see Appendix). These guides list gluten-free foods in various categories to aid your grocery

"Labeling laws are better… but it is still buyer beware."

shopping. And, remember manufacturers may change ingredients, so you have to constantly stay vigilant. Watch for the Food and Drug Administration's definition of "gluten-free" later in 2008 by checking these web sites: www.gluten.net, www.celiac.org; www.celiac.com, and www.glutenfreediet.ca.

Be prepared by planning ahead. This has all sorts of implications. Keep your own kitchen well stocked with the right ingredients so you can put together a meal at a moment's notice (see Gluten-Free Pantry, page 45).

Keep a bag of snacks (dried fruit, nuts, crackers, jerky, trail mix, etc.) on hand for when you're running errands, at a doctor's appointment, or at the kids' soccer games. Stick this bag in the glove box of your car or in your purse or briefcase. When you're hungry, munch on your *safe* foods rather giving in to temptation.

Stand up for your rights. Whether you're a schoolchild, a teenager, or an adult, you have a right to expect your food and the conditions under which it is served to be safe.

This means that you have a right to query the restaurant about its menu or your child's school about its lunch program. And, check out Section 504 of the Rehabilitation Act and the Individuals with Disabilities Education Act (IDEA) to learn more about your rights.

ഇ• Going against the Grain •ൠ
Alternative Flours for Gluten-Free Baking

Since you'll be using a blend of flours—rather than just a single flour—it is important to know the characteristics of the many flours you can choose for gluten-free baking.

Almond: Find almond meal or flour at www.BobsRedMill. Or, grind your own almond flour from blanched almond slivers, using your small coffee grinder. It has a high fat content, so refrigerate and use it within two months. Be sure to grind it as finely as possible for the best texture in baking but don't grind it too much or it will turn into almond butter.

Amaranth: Cultivated as a sacred food by the Aztecs for centuries, amaranth is not a grain but a relative of spinach and chard. For reasons unknown to us (rumor has it that Cortez forbade its cultivation), amaranth all but disappeared from the culinary horizon. Today, it can be obtained at natural food stores and by mail-order from www.nuworldamaranth.com.

Comparable to wheat in protein value, it has more calcium and amino acids—especially lysine—lacking in many common grains. Some describe the flavor as "woody"; others call it "grassy;" still others deem it "nutty." You will find the flavor stronger than that of rice flour, but not as strong as quinoa.

Amaranth's extremely small seeds are somewhat difficult to use, but the flour handles just like other flours. It slightly lengthens baking time and tends to brown a little faster than other flours. So, you want to take this into account when baking with it.

Combine it with other flours using up to 10 to 25% amaranth in flour blends, depending on the dish. Refrigerate or freeze (to avoid rancidity and flavor intensification) up to six months.

Amaranth Starch: Neutral-flavored starch made from amaranth; available at www.nuworldamaranth.com. Good replacement for cornstarch or potato starch in baking although it is more expensive. Store it in a dark, dry place.

Arrowroot: This is a neutral-flavored starch from the arrowroot plant grown in the West Indies. Dishes thickened with arrowroot remain crystal clear and somewhat shiny. It also can be substituted one-to-one for tapioca flour or cornstarch.

Because of this shiny look, arrowroot is best used as a thickener for fruit dishes or in dishes where its gloss gives the appearance of fat (even when there is no fat).

You might think of arrowroot as only a thickener, but in baking, arrowroot lightens gluten-free baked goods and adds some binding power as well.

Be sure to purchase arrowroot in the baking aisle of your local health food store where it is considerably cheaper than the little jars in the supermarket spice racks. Store it in a dark, dry place.

Barley: Although you see this ingredient listed on wheat-free products (often as barley flour or barley malt), it technically is a member of the wheat family and it contains gluten. Wheat-allergic persons and celiacs *should not* eat barley in any form. Barley is not used in this cookbook.

Buckwheat: Despite its name, buckwheat is not really wheat. Instead, it is related to rhubarb. Buckwheat flour is milled from unroasted groats (kernels) and graded as light, medium, or dark depending on the amount of remaining hulls. Typically...the darker the flour, the higher the lysine content. The trade-off, however, is a stronger flavor—which some find overpowering.

For baking, I favor lighter, unroasted buckwheat that has a light tan color with a yellowish cast. If you can't find the flour, grind unroasted groats in a blender or coffee grinder. The flavor will be somewhat musky but robust. Flour made from roasted buckwheat has an even stronger flavor.

Some people love buckwheat in pancakes; others find it too strong. Mixed with other flours, it produces delightful baked goods. I don't recommend it for thickening because it becomes somewhat gluey. Refrigerate for two months; freeze for 6 months.

Chestnut: Ground from chestnuts, this light tan flour is readily available at www.dowdandrogers.com which also offers baking mixes containing chestnut flour. (See Appendix.)

In baking, chestnut flour lends a silky texture and nutty flavor. Don't confuse it with water chestnut flour which is quite starchy. Also called marrons, chestnuts are lower in fat than other nuts. Chestnut flour should be used with other flours (up to 25% of the blend) in baking. It is commonly used in holiday baking, but I like to use it year-round because of the superior results it yields. Store it in dark, dry place.

Corn Flour and Corn Meal: Milled from corn kernels, the major difference lies in particle size. Use corn flour (the finer particles) in breads, desserts, pancakes, waffles, and homemade tortillas. Use cornmeal (coarser particles) for breading, in corn bread and muffins, and in polenta, where the larger particles lend crunch and texture.

Corn lends a distinct yet mild, nutty flavor to baked goods. If you can't find corn flour, grind cornmeal in your coffee grinder to the consistency of flour. Don't confuse corn flour with cornstarch (sometimes called corn flour in the UK).

Even if corn flour or corn meal is de-germinated, it's best to freeze rather than refrigerate them. This prevents condensation build-up in the package which can lead to mold.

Cornstarch: Highly refined with little nutritive value, cornstarch lightens baked goods and is an indispensable part of flour blends. It is snow-white and virtually flavorless, although more noticeable than arrowroot. It can be used interchangeably with potato starch.

As a thickener, cornstarch is used second only to wheat flour. However, it is often more desirable because it produces a smoother, more transparent texture and holds its thickening power better. Store it in a dark, dry place.

Flaxseeds and Flaxseed Meal: Flaxseeds are high in fiber and omega-3 fatty acids. They are a delicious way to add nutrients to gluten-free baked goods. You can buy flax meal already ground—or buy your own flaxseeds and grind them as you need them in a little coffee grinder. I freeze my flaxseeds and grind about a cup at a time, refrigerating the ground flax meal. I use it in baked goods (e.g., breads) and on my cereal to boost the nutrient content.

Garbanzo/Fava Bean or Garfava: This flour is made from a blend of garbanzo beans (also called chickpeas) and fava beans (or broad beans). This light yellowish-tan flour produces baked goods with a good rise, pleasing texture, and somewhat "beany" flavor.

Currently available from several manufacturers, look for it in health food stores or order directly from vendors (See Appendix). Store it in a dark, dry place.

Garbanzo (Chickpea): Unroasted chickpea flour (besan) lends a sweet, rich, slightly "beany" flavor to baked goods. It works best when blended with other flours, especially fava bean flour. Alone, chickpea flour lends a dry, delicate crumb to baked goods. Store it in a dark, dry place.

Mesquite: This is a relatively new flour ground from the pods of the mesquite tree. This sweet-tasting flour has a low-glycemic index and is high in protein. It is currently available as flour from www.casadefruta.com or www.therubyrange as dry mixes.

Millet: This flour lends a light-yellow tint to baked goods and produces a light, dry crumb with a smooth, thin crust. Very high in protein but—due to its high alkalinity—it is one of the easier grains to digest.

Millet performs best when blended with other flours, comprising no more than 25% of the flour blend. It also makes a great hot breakfast cereal in its whole grain form.

Purchase millet flour in small amounts because it can quickly become bitter and rancid. Refrigerate, tightly covered, for two months.

Montina (Indian ricegrass): This flour, developed from Indian ricegrass, is grown in Montana (www.montina.com). Darker in color, it makes dark, hearty baked goods with a definite "chew."

Relatively high in protein, it works best blended with other, lighter flours. Use as 25% of the flour blend. It is particularly good in hearty breads and muffins because it makes them resemble whole wheat versions. Refrigerate, tightly covered.

Oat: Oats do not inherently contain gluten, but the danger of cross-contamination with wheat in the fields and during processing makes the presence of gluten possible in regular oats. Today, we have pure, uncontaminated gluten-free oats available at www.bobsredmill.com, www.creamhillestates.com, www.giftsofnature.net, www.glutenfreeoats.com, and www.onlyoats.com. Ninety-eight percent of persons with celiac disease can eat gluten-free oats but check with your physician first just in case you're one of the two percent who don't tolerate any type of oats. For a discussion of oats in the gluten-free diet, go to www.gluten.net or www.glutenfreediet.ca.

Baked goods made with oats turn out especially moist and flavorful with a cake-like crumb. But oat flour can be heavy in baking, so it is usually combined with other flours (such as sorghum flour or rice flour or potato starch) to make a palatable product. For best results, use oat flour as 25 to 33% of the flour blend.

You can buy oat flour or grind rolled oats into flour with a small coffee grinder. Store oat groats on the pantry shelf, but freeze oat flour for up to four months.

Pecan (Flour or Meal): Ground from pecans, this is really meal rather than flour. Pecan meal is often used in flourless cakes, accompanied by several eggs for leavening. If using with other flours, pecan meal can comprise up to 25% of the flour blend.

Due to the skins, pecan meal lends a slight nutty taste and an interesting texture to baked goods. Pecans have a fairly high fat content. Therefore, ground meal turns rancid quickly. To avoid this, buy whole pecans and grind in a food processor, as needed.

Refrigerate whole pecans for 6 months. Pecan meal should be frozen, tightly covered, for no more than two months.

Potato Flour: Made from whole potatoes that have been cooked and then ground, this heavy flour is seldom used in large quantities for baking. In small quantities, it balances flour blends by adding weight, body, and "chewiness," e.g., in cookies and yeast breads. Like tapioca flour, it hardens the crust of baked goods.

Off-white in color, potato flour has a stronger taste than potato starch. Buy small amounts; use quickly. Since the flavor deteriorates quickly, refrigerate in airtight container for up to two months.

Potato Starch: Made from only the starch of potatoes (not the whole potato), this fine, white powder lightens baked goods. Because it may lump during storage, whisk before using.

Potato starch usually makes up a portion (usually no more than 33% but sometimes more—depending on the recipe) of flour blends, but is rarely used alone in baking. It can be used 1:1 in place of cornstarch. Because it has little or no protein or fat, potato starch can be stored on a dark, dry pantry shelf.

Quinoa: Quinoa is an ancient grain originally grown high in the Andes of Peru. A source of high quality protein and lysine, it is one of the most nutritious grains on earth. Totally gluten-free, it is not really a grain but a seed related to lamb's quarter, spinach, and beets. It produces a delicate, cake-like crumb in baking.

Although quinoa flour is available in health food stores and by mail-order, it is actually made from quinoa grains which you can grind yourself. And, quinoa flour should be mixed with other flours for successful baking, preferably making up no more than 15 to 20% of the flour blend. This means you'll use small amounts of quinoa flour, so grind it as you need it in your coffee grinder.

Unlike most imported quinoa, domestic quinoa isn't always rinsed of its saponin, a bitter natural insect repellent. So, rinse the grains at least 3 times or until the water runs clear. If you're grinding your own, be sure to dry the kernels first. Also, if cross-contamination is a concern, purchase the imported brands (e.g., Inca Organics or Ancient Harvest) only. Some domestically grown quinoa may be grown in close proximity to wheat. Refrigerate in airtight container.

Rice (Brown or White): Perhaps the most common of wheat substitutes, it lends a light, somewhat sandy texture to baked goods. To reduce this sandiness, mix it with other flours. The flavor of rice is neutral, and rice is one of the least allergenic foods on earth—making it a natural choice to replace wheat.

Both brown and white rice flour are milled from the broken hulls of rice kernels. Unfortunately, this reduces the nutritional content to mostly starch because the bran layers are milled away. But these "layers" are available as rice polish or rice bran (see below). Try adding these rice by-products to your baked goods to increase fiber and nutrient content. Refrigerate brown rice flour to prevent rancidity.

Rice Bran: The outside layer of the rice kernel that is removed to make brown rice, it contains the bran and part of the rice germ. Dark in color, it adds fiber and protein to baked goods. For breads or muffins, use 1/4 cup per recipe. Find it at natural food stores; order from www.ener-g.com. Refrigerate to prevent rancidity.

Rice Polish: This is the portion of the brown rice kernel removed in the process of making white rice. It contains part of the rice germ and bran. High in fiber, it is light in color (unlike rice bran which is darker in color). Find it at natural food stores; order it from www.ener-g.com. Refrigerate to prevent rancidity.

Sorghum: Some believe that the flour made from this nutritious grain tastes the closest to wheat. It is light tan in color, not gritty, and works very well in baking. It is an excellent way to introduce more protein and variety into the gluten-free diet.

Sometimes called milo, early varieties were grown only for cattle feed (as on the Nebraska farm where I was raised), but today's versions are grown for what's called table or food or white sorghum. Faintly sweet and somewhat dry, sorghum works best when blended with other flours, making up no more than 25 to 30% of the total—although some recipes can handle up to 50%.

It is available at your local health food store or directly from several manufacturers: Authentic Foods, Bob's Red Mill, Ener-G Foods, and as whole grains and flour from Twin Valley Mills. (See Appendix.) It can be stored at room temperature in a dark, dry place.

Sorghum Grits: Available directly where it's grown from Twin Valley Mills (www.twinvalleymills.com), this is a nutritious, delicious way to add fiber to our gluten-free diets. Because it includes the outer hulls of the sorghum kernel, its coarseness may vary. I use it to make hot breakfast cereal.

Soy (whole or defatted) Soy flour is made from soybeans and brings wonderful qualities to gluten-free baking—including a moist, fine crumb and a smooth, hard crust. It works especially well in baked goods containing nuts, fruit, or chocolate. Like all other gluten-free flours, soy must be combined with other flours for best results—both because it has no gluten and because it has a slight "beany" flavor. Soybeans are very hard so grinding your own soy flour is not possible.

Due to its high fat and protein content, it has a short shelf life and should be purchased in small quantities. Refrigerate soy flour in a tightly covered container for up to two months.

Spelt: This sweet, nutty grain produces flour that is often used in place of wheat flour. However, gluten-sensitive people *must not* use this flour because it contains gluten—albeit less of it. You'll find many cookbooks with recipes for using spelt in baked goods, so I don't offer any here. Again, if you're gluten-sensitive or have celiac disease or wheat allergies—*do not eat spelt*.

Sweet Potato: This flour is hard to find, except in some specialty stores and by mail from www.ener-g.com. Since sweet potatoes are one of the least allergenic foods on earth (they belong to the morning glory family), this flour may be a good choice for persons with multiple sensitivities.

Sweet potato flour produces baked goods with a great taste and texture. Its yellowy-orange color is visible in light-colored baked goods so use it in chocolate or darkly-colored baked items such as spice cakes for best results. Its faint sweetness will affect gravies and savory sauces, so it is best reserved for sweeter items. Refrigerate, tightly covered.

Sweet Rice: Also called "sticky rice", it is made from a particular kind of rice called "glutinous" rice (although it contains no wheat gluten). This bland, starchy flour has stronger binding qualities than other rice flours. Manufacturers recommend using it in muffins, breads, and cakes. My experience suggests using it as a small part (perhaps 25 to 30%) of the total flour blend.

Sweet rice flour works particularly well in items that require a great of elasticity and pliability such as pie crusts. Sweet rice flour really shines as a thickener in savory dishes because it produces a nice, creamy sauce and inhibits separation of the sauce when chilled or frozen. If you can't find it at your natural food store, order it from www.ener-g.com. Store it in a dark, dry place.

Tapioca (also called tapioca starch or manioc, which is used in Chebe® bread): This neutral flavored starch is made from the cassava plant, cultivated in South America and Florida. It is widely available in natural food stores.

Tapioca flour lightens gluten-free baked goods, lends a "chewy" texture, and encourages browning with a crispy crust. Used in a similar manner to arrowroot, it usually makes up about 20% of the total flour mix. Store in a dark, dry place.

Teff: Grown in Ethiopa for centuries, this tiny grain wasn't introduced to the U.S. until the 1980's. It is so small that it takes 150 grains to equal one kernel of wheat, although it is not related to wheat at all.

It produces a sweet, nutty almost malt-flavored flour that works especially well in cookies, cakes, and quick breads. Experts caution against using it in yeast breads because its own symbiotic yeast has a negative effect on the yeast you add to leaven the bread.

Like other gluten-free, yet highly nutritious grains such as quinoa or amaranth, teff should be combined with other flours for success in baking—comprising perhaps 25 to 30% of the flour blend.

The teff flour you will find in health food stores is darker and most likely grown in Caldwell, ID. There is also a light-colored version as well. The grains are so small you won't be able to grind the flour yourself. If you can't find teff in your natural food store, order it from www.teffco.com. Store in a dark, dry, cool place.

Wild Rice: Wild rice is not actually rice at all, but a grain. And, it is richer in protein, minerals, and B vitamins, and higher in carbohydrates than wheat. It lends a rich, nutty flavor to baked goods, and—as with all gluten-free flours—it needs to be blended with other flours for best results—making up perhaps 25 to 30% of the total blend of flours.

You can grind your own wild rice flour using a small coffee grinder. Grind it as you need it, and if you have any left over, store it in the refrigerator, covered, for up to two months.

Storage of Gluten-Free Flours
I prefer to store flours in glass jars rather than in plastic bags or plastic containers. I use wide-mouthed jars so I can easily measure the flour right over the top of the container, scraping the excess right back into the jar. Use the method that works best for you. If you freeze your flour, bring it to room temperature before using.

Notes on Gluten-Free Flours

☙• Substitutes for Wheat as a Thickener •❧

Many of us learned to cook using wheat flour as a thickener in gravies, soups, and sauces. Other starches and flours can thicken certain foods but each alternative has certain strengths. Use the following information to choose among them.

In place of **1 tablespoon of wheat flour**, use the following:

Ingredient/Amount	Traits	Suggested Uses
Agar (Kanten) 1 ½ tsp.	Follow package directions. Colorless, flavor-less. Sets at room temperature. Gels acidic liquids. Thin sauces need less.	Puddings, pie fillings, gelatin desserts, ice cream, glazes, cheese. Holds moisture and improves texture in pastry products.
Arrowroot 1 ½ tsp.	Mix with cold water before using. Thickens at lower temperature than wheat flour or cornstarch; better for eggs or sauces that shouldn't be boiled. Add during last 5 minutes of cooking. Serve right away after thickening. Clear, shiny. Semi-soft when cool.	Any food requiring clear, shiny sauce, but good for egg or starch dishes where high heat is undesirable. Gives appearance of oil even when none used.\n\nDon't overcook or sauce will thin somewhat.
Bean Flour (chickpea) 1 Tbsp.	Produces yellowish, rich-looking sauce.	Soups, stews, gravies. Slight bean taste.
Cornstarch 1 ½ tsp.	Mix with cold liquid before use. Stir just to boiling. Transparent, shiny sauce. Slight starchy flavor. Thicker and rigid when cool.	Puddings, pie fillings, fruit sauces, soups. Gives appearance of oil even when none used.
Gelatin Powder (unflavored) 1 ½ tsp.	Dissolve in cold water. Then heat until clear before using.	Cheesecakes, gelatin salads, puddings, aspics. Won't gel acidic fruit such as pineapple.

↳• Substitutes for Wheat as a Thickener •↲
(continued)

Ingredient/Amount	Traits	Suggested Uses
Guar Gum 1 ½ tsp.	Mix with liquid before use. High fiber can act as laxative.	Especially good for rice flour recipes.
Kudzu (kuzu) Powder 1 ½ tsp.	Dissolve in cold water before using. Odorless, tasteless. Makes transparent, smooth sauces with soft consistency.	Puddings, pie fillings, and gelled preparations. May need to experiment to find exact amount to use.
Potato Starch 1 ½ tsp.	Mix with cold liquid before using.	Soups, stews, gravies.
Rice Flour (brown or white) 1 Tbsp.	Mix with cold water before using. Grainy texture. Consistency the same hot or cold.	Soups, stews, gravies.
Sweet Rice Flour 1 Tbsp.	Excellent thickening agent.	Sauces such as vegetable sauces.
Tapioca Flour 1 ½ Tbsp.	Mix with cold water before using. Add during last 5 minutes of cooking to avoid rubbery consistency. Makes transparent, shiny sauce. Thick, soft gel when cool.	Soups, stews, gravies, potato dishes.
Quick-Cooking Tapioca (pre-cooked) 2 tsp.	Mix with fruit. Let stand 15 minutes before baking.	Fruit pies, cobblers, and tapioca pudding.
Xanthan Gum 1 tsp.	Mix with dry ingredients first, then add to recipe.	Puddings, salad dressings, and gravies.

ରେ୍ The Name Game ୧·ଆ
Where Gluten Lurks in Your Kitchen

Many people tell of their joy at finally learning the source of their distress—gluten. Eventually, however, they express dismay at discovering that gluten is *everywhere.*

For me, it was like walking into the kitchen and finding that every cupboard door was locked. The refrigerator door, too. I had a kitchen full of food, yet most of it was no longer safe. Of course, I knew that breads, bagels, pasta, crackers, cake, cookies—the obvious gluten stuff—was off-limits.

What I didn't understand is that gluten isn't limited to the obvious foods. I was surprised to learn that other common foods were suspect, as well. This included old-time favorites like the cream of mushroom soup in all my casseroles, the soy sauce that I liberally added to Asian dishes, and even the licorice candy that I *thought* was good for me because it was low fat!

One good resource for gluten-free newbies is the Quick Start Diet Guide, published jointly by two national associations: the Gluten Intolerance Group of North America and the Celiac Disease Foundation available in a downloadble pdf format at www.gluten.net. In simple, easy-to-understand terms, it outlines what's allowed and what's forbidden on the gluten-free diet (see Associations in the Appendix for addresses).

Reading Labels
Yes, gluten is *everywhere.* And, if you accept the fact that gluten can lurk in just about anything, you'll be safer than if you presume that your favorite food couldn't possibly contain this dreaded protein.

So, how do you know? What do you look for on labels? Well, let's start out with how to read labels.

The Federal Government now requires a consistent design for labels on packaged foods. This helps consumers compare foods and make informed decisions. Here is a sample label. Although it is fictitious, it illustrates several points that are important to know whether or you're gluten-free or not.

1. Serving sizes are often much smaller than we realize. And, a serving size isn't necessarily large enough to satisfy your hunger. In this era of "super-size" food, most people eat more than one serving.

2. Fat contains more than twice as many calories as carbohydrates or protein.

3. Information from these labels helps you balance your food choices by comparing your daily intake with the recommendation.

Serving Size
Based on average serving size designated by industry.

Number of Servings
Total product divided by

average serving size.

Divide Calories from Fat (110) by Calories (250) to get percent calories from fat.

Label Information
Highlights nutrients required by law: Vitamins A & C, Calcium, and Iron. If food product is fortified, that information is also shown.

% Daily Value
How this food fits into a daily diet of 2000 calories.

Daily Values Footnote
Based on current nutrition recommendations.

Calories Per Gram
Caloric value of energy-producing nutrients.

Nutrition Facts

Serving Size 1 cup (228g)
Servings Per Container 2

Amount Per Serving
Calories 250 Calories from Fat 110

	% Daily Value
Total Fat 12g	18%
Saturated Fat 3g	15%
Cholesterol 30 mg	10%
Sodium 470 mg	20%
Total Carbohydrates 31g	10%
Dietary Fiber 0g	0%
Sugar 5g	
Protein 5g	

Vitamin A 4%	Vitamin C 2%
Calcium 20%	Iron 4%

Percent Daily Values are based on a 2000 calorie diet. Your daily values may be higher or lower depending on your calorie needs.

	Calories	2000	2500
Total Fat	Less Than	65g	80g
Sat. Fat	Less Than	20g	25g
Cholesterol	Less Than	300mg	300mg
Sodium	Less Than	2400mg	2400mg
Total Carbohydrate		300mg	375mg
Dietary Fiber		25g	30g

Calories Per Gram
Fat 9   Carbohydrate 4   Protein 4

Note: Over time, the format of this nutrition label may change, so regard this example as illustrative only.

Guess What's Coming to Dinner!

In addition to the nutrition label, the Food & Drug Administration (FDA) requires that standardized food items have a list of ingredients. This list tells us a lot about what is in the food—but it doesn't necessarily tell us as much as we *need* to know.

Basically, ingredients are listed in order of magnitude—those weighing most are listed first, followed in descending order by those occurring in increasingly smaller and smaller amounts.

For example, from the following ingredient list—sugar, flour, butter, baking powder, cinnamon, and salt—you can see that sugar is the largest ingredient in this food and salt is the smallest.

Gluten-Free Labeling

As noted earlier in this book, since January, 2006, labels of food manufactured in the U.S. are required to clearly state the ingredients—in plain English—if they contain any of the eight major allergens: wheat, dairy, soy, eggs, peanuts, tree nuts, fish, and shellfish.

This labeling makes food shopping easier but, as you choose foods for your gluten-free pantry, you should carefully read the labels of *everything* you buy, each time you buy it—even if you've bought the item many times before, are familiar with the manufacturer, and have confidence in that company. You must continue to read labels because manufacturers might change ingredients or manufacturing procedures. You should also read the labels of foods that you wouldn't expect to contain wheat, or that didn't contain it in the past, because things can change there as well.

In the meantime, be vigilant. Stick to those brands that are confirmed gluten-free by the manufacturer. However, the use of the term "gluten-free" is voluntary by manufacturers so not all gluten-free foods will be so labeled. And, as we go to press with this book in June, 2008, there is not a single definition of gluten-free.

In late 2008, the FDA will issue its definition of gluten-free. Go to www.gluten.net, www.celiac.com, www.celiac.org, or www.glutenfreediet.ca for the final ruling. In the meantime, use handy reference guides to help you determine which products are safe, such as those from the Celiac Sprue Association, Clan Thompson, or the Essential Gluten-Free Grocery Guide (see Resources in Appendix). These guides list gluten-free foods by category and brand, making grocery shopping much easier. But always read the label every time you make a purchase.

To further help consumers identify safe foods, the Gluten-Free Certification Organization (www.gfco.org), a branch of the Gluten Intolerance Group) certifies companies as gluten-free and authorizes them to display a certification logo on the food item, as does the Celiac Sprue Association (www.csaceliacs.org). Companies that don't use these logos don't necessarily manufacture unsafe foods, but these logos are yet another tool for you to use when you shop.

The Food Allergy & Anaphylaxis Network (FAAN) sends out notices to its members on ingredient changes, mislabeling, and manufacturing accidents in which food is unintentionally contaminated with known allergens such as wheat. While it is a very worthwhile association to join for many reasons, this benefit alone makes it money well spent.

Unexpected or Confusing Sources of Gluten
Gluten is present in *well-known* grains such as barley, rye, and spelt. But it's also present in more exotic, less well-known grains such as triticale, kamut, einkorn, and farro. Don't be misled by labels that tout these grains as gluten-free. They're still part of the wheat family and contain gluten. And, yes—white bread and sprouted bread contain wheat and, therefore, they contain gluten.

Be careful about the term "wheat-free." This term is used frequently on foods that nonetheless contain a member of the wheat family such as barley, kamut, or spelt—or regular oats, which *may* be contaminated with gluten. The food must say "gluten-free" to be safe for us.

Even though pure, uncontaminated gluten-free oats are available, this doesn't mean that oat-containing foods are gluten-free. Unless the label explicitly says "made with gluten-free oats" you should assume that the product uses regular oats and is not gluten-free—unless you verify the food with the manufacturer.

Gluten might not be in the ingredients, but your food may be prepared in the same receptacle or manufacturing line as gluten-containing foods. Many manufacturers now put the phrase "made in a plant that also processes wheat" (or something similar) on the package. This is confusing, but at this moment it is actually possible to manufacture products on shared equipment and still produce food that can carry a gluten-free label if the conditions are carefully controlled and the equipment is thoroughly cleaned between runs. Once the specific definition of "gluten-free" is determined by the FDA in late 2008 we'll have a standard to guide manufacturers and hopefully some of this confusion will subside.

The list below alerts you to unexpected sources of gluten; it doesn't suggest that gluten is illegally hiding anywhere. This list is not all-inclusive, it may change, and it pertains to foods manufactured in the United States. For more information, see "Tricky Ingredients" by Ann Whelan in the Fall, 2007, issue of *Gluten-Free Living* magazine. Finally, be sure to read labels each and every time you make purchase and, remember—if you are ever in doubt about any food, *don't eat it!*

• **Alcoholic Beverages:** Avoid regular beer, ale, and lager, but experts say that distilled spirits are safe (gin, vodka, whisky, etc.) because gluten cannot survive the distillation process. Wine is generally safe, although reactions to sulfite preservatives can sometimes occur. Certain brands of hard cider are gluten-free, such as Woodchuck. Gluten-free beer is made by several companies including Anheuser-Busch Redbridge, Bard's Tale, Discover, New Grist, and Ramapo Valley..... to name just a few.

• **Beverages:** Avoid Postum and Ovaltine since they may contain barley malt for flavoring. Also avoid any beverage that lists barley malt, grains, or oats (such as oat milk) on the label unless you can verify that the grains are gluten-free.

• **Candy:** Gluten may be an unsuspected ingredient (for example, licorice contains wheat flour). It might also be used in the shaping or handling of candy (such as dusting conveyor belts to prevent sticking).

• **Caramel Color:** In North America, this is made from corn and should not be a problem. Be careful about products made outside North America, however, because they *could* contain gluten.

• **Cereal:** Avoid cereals with wheat, rye, oats, barley, spelt, triticale and kamut or those flavored with barley malt or malt syrup. Cereals made solely from amaranth, brown rice, buckwheat, flax, Montina, millet, rice, quinoa, sorghum, soy, and teff—with no gluten-containing additions—are safe.

• **Citric acid:** Made from fermented corn, beets, sugar, molasses, or wheat and is so highly purified that no wheat could be present.

• **Coffee:** Pure coffee is safe, but coffee substitutes usually contain wheat or barley.

• **Condiments and Baking Ingredients:** Pure spices are gluten-free. Check labels, especially on seasonings or seasoning blends, certain dried or prepared mustards, salad dressings, soy sauces, or prepared sauces. Look for gluten-free versions of these ingredients. For example, wheat-free tamari is a safe form of soy sauce. Some dry mustard powder (e.g, Coleman's) may contain wheat flour, so use Durkee or McCormick dry mustard or grind your own mustard seeds with a small coffee grinder.

Salad dressings are usually gluten-free, but I have seen some thickened with wheat flour. Lea & Perrins Worcestershire sauce is gluten-free in the U.S., but not in Canada. The area of condiments and baking ingredients is huge, so consult the product lists from CSA/USA, Clan Thompson, or the Essential Gluten-Free Grocery Guide (see Appendix.).

• **Dairy Products:** Malted milk should be avoided as well as malted milk mixes.

• **Desserts and Other Sweets:** Check labels on cake decorations and marzipan because they *may* contain wheat flour as a thickener or binder.

• **Distilled Vinegar:** Vinegar made from wine, rice, or cider is safe for gluten-free diets. Previously, the accepted wisdom was to avoid distilled vinegar because it *might* contain gluten. Today, experts say that distilled vinegar is safe for gluten-free diets because wheat is rarely used in the distillation process and, even if it was, the gluten peptides could not survive the distillation process. Avoid malt vinegar because barley malt flavoring is added in after the distillation process. The single word "vinegar" on a label indicates apple cider vinegar. Typically, distilled white vinegar is made from corn. Nonetheless, it's possible that vinegar may cause reactions that are unrelated to gluten in some people—most likely due to sensitivity to vinegar itself (perhaps the yeast?) and is solved by avoiding it.

• **Extracts and Flavorings:** Extracts such as vanilla are safe for gluten-free diets because, like the vinegar-making process, the gluten peptides can't survive the distillation process. Malt flavoring is made from barley and should be avoided. Imitation vanilla is a synthetic product made from vanillin, the main flavoring component of vanilla, and may be made from wood pulp by-products—again not an issue for the gluten-sensitive.

• **Hydrolyzed Vegetable Protein (HVP):** Can be made from corn, soy, peanut, or wheat, but the source will be on the label.

• **Meats:** Be wary of any meat that has been breaded or processed in a way that fillers might be used such as sausage, luncheon meats, or hot dogs—unless the product says gluten-free.

• **Modified Food Starch:** Generally speaking, modified food starch is corn if made in the U.S. although it *could* be made from tapioca, potato, rice or (rarely) wheat if made outside the U.S. Manufacturers must list the source.

• **Pasta**: Choose Oriental rice noodles, bean threads, and commercial pasta made from bean, rice, corn, tapioca, or potato starch flour. Be sure to read labels since some pasta is made from a mixture of flours that may also include wheat or a member of the wheat family. For example, although Eden Foods makes a 100% buckwheat pasta, most buckwheat pasta is blended with wheat.

• **Soups and Chowders:** Many canned soups, soup mixes, and bouillon cubes or granules are made with wheat, so check the labels.

• **Spices and Seasonings**: See **Condiments and Baking Ingredients**.

• **Vegetables:** Avoid vegetables that are breaded, creamed, or scalloped because this usually involves wheat flour or bread crumbs made from wheat.

• **Yeast:** Baker's yeast is gluten-free. Common brands such as Red Star and Fleischman are gluten free. Nutritional yeast (a supplement) is gluten-free. Brewer's yeast (a by-product of the brewing industry) may be gluten-free, unless it is a by-product of brewing beer, so check with the manufacturer. Autolyzed yeast, commonly used as a food flavoring, is generally gluten-free.

This section is based on my own investigation and experiences with gluten-free ingredients as well as information from *Gluten-Free Living* Magazine, *Quick Start Diet Guide* by the Gluten Intolerance Group and the Celiac Disease Foundation; *Gluten-Free Diet: a Comprehensive Resource Guide*, Expanded Edition, 2006, by Shelley Case, BSc, RD; and the Clan Thompson Celiac Food SmartList.

☙ Notes on Gluten-Free Ingredients ❧

☞ Get Going—Gluten-Free ☜
Traveling Well without Gluten

For those of us with sand in our shoes, wanderlust, or a job that requires being on the road… travel can present a challenge to our gluten-free lifestyle. Fortunately, it is possible to see the world and still avoid gluten, with a little advance planning on your part.

There are many wonderful articles and web sites that can give you information on how to avoid gluten while traveling, such as www.allergyfreepassport.com. What I'll do here is to tell you how *I* travel well without gluten.

Planning Ahead
Knowing where I'm going, the type of restaurants available, and how knowledgeable these restaurants will be are all key factors in planning ahead. I query friends, colleagues, and even strangers to find out about my destination. I keep files, especially for foreign countries, so information is ready when wanderlust strikes again.

Traveling in (Gluten-free) Style
I travel lightly. That usually means one suitcase plus a large, light-weight nylon bag that doubles as a food bag en route to my destination—and as a container for souvenirs on the way home.

For example, on a recent trip to Europe here's what I took for snacks. These ideas work for domestic travel, too.

Snacks (packed in individual plastic, recloseable snack bags)
- crackers (Edward & Sons or Mary's Gone Crackers)
- nuts (pecans, almonds, walnuts)
- seeds (roasted sunflower seeds and pumpkin seeds)
- dried fruit (apricots; cranberries; dried plums; I dry my own apple rings.)
- fruit leather
- bars (Lara bars or Enjoy Life bars)
- fresh fruit such as apples, grapes, bananas, etc. However, I only take enough fruit for the first day because it's heavy and spoils quickly without refrigeration.

For bread with meals and at breakfast, I carry the Food for Life or LaTortilla Factory tortilla wraps in their own bag or I vacuum-seal the following with my Food-Saver by Tilia (after freezing the food first):
- homemade muffins
- store-bought bread (Ener-G Foods has two-slice packets)
- savory cheese biscotti

Breakfast
For breakfast, I make my favorite Granola (page 107) and package it in snack bags. If you add your favorite nuts, M&Ms, and more dried fruit it becomes a great Trail Mix for snacks. I also take other cereals that travel well such as Nutty Rice, Nutty Corn, Nutty Flax, or granola, all from Enjoy Life Foods (www.enjoylifenaturalbrands.com).

I also take plastic bags of hot cereal (such as Cream of Rice or Cream of Buckwheat or Ancient Harvest quinoa flakes) and mix them with hot water in my hotel room. I carry a small "infuser" to heat the water or, in some cases, hotel rooms are equipped with coffee makers or microwave ovens that can heat water.

Being a fairly early riser and a hearty breakfast eater, I often eat fruit or cereal in my hotel room and then join my travel companion(s) in the dining room later for a traditional breakfast of eggs, bacon, and potatoes.

I always have a plastic toaster bag (www.allergygrocer.com or www.toastitbags.com) with me to toast bread without fear of contamination.

Lunch
If sandwiches are the only choice on the menu, I sometimes just order the sandwich fillings (such as sliced turkey, lettuce, tomato, etc.) and construct a sandwich using my own bread or crackers—or eat the filling separately. I package the bread in plastic snack bags or—if I'm traveling for several days—vacuum pack the bread while it's frozen. I've never had a restaurant prohibit this. If they ask, I simply say I can't eat regular bread and let it go at that.

My favorite (safe) lunch, however, is a salad with plain grilled chicken or fish on top—and plenty of vegetables. If the salad dressing is questionable, I just use oil and vinegar or fresh lemon juice. Many upscale restaurants make their own salad dressing and so I can query the chef about the ingredients. I ask the chef to omit croutons and any batter-fried additions like goat cheese rounds.

I tend to avoid soups unless I am certain they are not thickened with wheat. The only exceptions are lentil or bean soups that *usually* don't need a thickener.

Dinner

I'm very fond of fish, so I often order it in restaurants—preferably grilled. I like potatoes or rice, but I often ask that they be replaced with vegetables. That way, I'm avoiding the issue of how the potatoes or rice are prepared and I come closer to meeting my quota of vegetables for the day.

The safest thing is to make sure my fish (or pork chops, which I'm also fond of) are "naked." That is, they have no breading, flour-based spice rubs, or flour-based marinades. Usually, if you just ask for grilled meat there is nothing on it except salt and pepper—but always ask. Some people carry small jars of their favorite spice mix or rub and just sprinkle it on their food after it is served.

If possible, ask for an empty refrigerator in your hotel room and, if possible, a coffee maker. That way, you can chill what needs to be chilled and heat water if necessary.

Travel to Foreign Countries

I love to visit grocery stores and health food stores in foreign countries. In Germany, I discovered the Reformhaus stores which carry many wonderful gluten-free baked goods. On a recent visit, I filled my car trunk with an array of wonderful foods and ate safely and deliciously for two weeks!

While in Italy with the *Living Without* magazine tour in 2000, we discovered the wonderful Dr. Schar products. Our Tuscan chef introduced us to delicious breads, crackers, pasta, and baking mixes. They are available through www.glutensolutions.com or www.glutino.com. When I toured northern Italy in mid-2005, we had Dr. Schar pasta and bread sent to our hotels so we always had fresh bread and all the pasta we could eat.

On my many trips to Japan recently to conduct gluten-free seminars, I was fortunate to have the assistance of English-speaking colleagues. Otherwise, I could not decipher the menus at traditional Japanese restaurants. However, staying at an American hotel that serves American food alongside Japanese dishes and that has an English-speaking staff eases travel in Japan.

Speaking of foreign languages, you would be wise to invest in a set of wallet cards in the language of the country you're visiting. These cards list the foods you must avoid in the language of the country you're visiting. *Living Without* magazine offers cards in a variety of different languages (www.livingwithout.com) as does www.allergyfreepassport.com.

Celiacs Travel Together
If you're unwilling or unable to travel alone, look to Bob & Ruth's Travel Club for help. They sponsor trips to exotic places all over the world, often on cruise ships. Most meals are eaten on board the ship and are all gluten-free, so there's no worry about safety or contamination. However, they also offer U.S. trips and assure you a totally gluten-free travel experience (see Appendix).

The important thing is not to let your gluten-free diet keep you at home. Some people even purchase recreational vehicles so they can travel with their own kitchen close at hand. Others enjoy camping. Still others seek lodging where kitchenettes are available. If any of these options work for you, fine. If travel is important to you, you'll find a way to do it that's safe for you.

⚜• The Gluten-Free Kitchen •⚜

S ome people are naturally comfortable in the kitchen. Others are bothered, baffled, and bewildered at the thought of preparing their own food…with strange ingredients, no less.

I was fortunate to have a mother who cooked *all* of our meals and that gave me the opportunity to observe her in the kitchen. Funny… I seem to do things the same way she did. And, interestingly, my son—who is a good cook and very skilled in the kitchen—does a lot of things just like me.

But, even if your mother didn't cook or you didn't take Home Economics in high school, this chapter will assure your success in the kitchen.

Getting Started
• First, read the recipe completely to make sure you have all the ingredients you'll need, along with the right pans and utensils. This may sound overly simple, but you'd be surprised at how many people call me when they're in the middle of preparing the recipe saying, "Help… I'm baking a (cake, etc.) and just realized I don't have (ingredient/utensil/pan)." What should I do?" Planning ahead is critical to success.

• Organize the ingredients. I place all the ingredients on one side of the counter and, after I use them, I transfer them to the other side of the counter. This way, interruptions such as phone calls, the doorbell, or other distractions won't make me forget the xanthan gum—or add the salt twice.

• Measure correctly. Before measuring your (gluten-free) flour, stir it with a whisk. As flour sits in canisters over time, it tends to settle and become more compacted. Stirring aerates it. Lightly spoon it into a dry measuring cup and level with a knife. Don't shake or tap cup and don't force flour down into the cup. Not following these tips can yield up to 20% more flour than you need and is one of the chief causes of baking failures.

• Use liquid measuring cups to measure liquids. How do you know which cups are right? Liquid measuring cups usually have a pour spout and are plastic or glass so you can see through them. Set the measuring cup on the counter-top and bend down to read it at eye-level. Never use dry measuring cups to measure liquids. This can yield up to 20% more liquid and can ruin a recipe.

• Use real measuring spoons—not spoons from the silverware drawer. Make sure measuring spoons are a standard size from a reputable manufacturer. A major cooking magazine compared tablespoons from different manufacturers and found that capacities ranged from 9 to 14 grams each. That makes a huge difference when you're measuring several tablespoons.

• Preheat oven for at least 20 minutes to make sure it reaches the specified temperature. Some ovens take even longer.

• Use middle oven rack, unless directed otherwise. Place baking pan in center of rack so heated air can circulate freely around it.

• Cool baked goods in pan 10 to 15 minutes. Then remove them by running knife along edge of the pan. Finish cooling on a rack. To avoid sogginess, don't leave baked goods in the pan longer than 15 minutes.

• Unless otherwise specified in the recipe, you can assume that:
  • Butter is unsalted; you may use buttery spread, e.g., Earth Balance
  • Eggs are large (each should be not quite ¼ cup in volume)
  • Sugar is granulated white—not brown, raw, or turbinado sugar, unless specified otherwise in the ingredient list

• Follow the recipe as directed. This means *exactly* as directed. I've already made the ingredient substitutions for you. Don't make any others, unless you know what you're doing.

Following the recipe also means using the right utensil or pan. If the recipe says "whisk" then you should use a whisk, not a spatula. If it says to use a food processor to mix the dough, it will blend better than if you use an electric mixer. The reason is that a food processor distributes liquid more quickly and evenly— making a smoother, more consistent dough.

Pan size is also important. If you use an 11 x 7-inch pan instead of a 8-inch square pan, the batter is distributed over a larger area. As a result, it will probably bake in a shorter period of time, won't rise as high, and might burn more quickly.

• Use the oven temperature specified in the recipe. And, use an oven thermometer to be sure your oven is actually heated to the *right* temperature. Some ovens need to be calibrated and not all ovens operate the same way. Be sure to preheat the oven so that it reaches the right temperature *before* you start baking.

• Start checking doneness a few minutes before the time specified in the recipe. There are so many variables that can affect the baking time (oven temperature variations, pan size, ingredients, temperature of ingredients, humidity, ambient temperature, etc.). The wise cook knows to use other techniques to judge doneness such as an instant-read thermometer, the appearance of the baked item, and the physical feel (e.g., crispness of crust when tapped).

Substitute Saviors

We've all had it happen. We're ready to bake, yet we're missing one critical ingredient. There isn't time to run to the store. Help!!!

Take heart. There is usually a good substitute for the missing ingredient. Use the same amount, unless indicated otherwise. Substitutes may alter the flavor and appearance of baked items.

Instead of...	Use same amount of...
Almond meal/flour	Finely ground pecans, walnuts, cashews, or pumpkin seeds (use small coffee grinder or food processor to grind whole nuts into meal or flour)
Rice flour	Sorghum, garbanzo/fava bean flour
Butter	Buttery spread or margarine (not diet)
Cornstarch	Arrowroot, potato starch, lotus root, or amaranth starch
Milk	Nut, rice, soy, or hazelnut beverage
Milk Powder	Non-dairy powders by Better Than Milk, or Vance's Dari-Free (not Carnation)
Potato starch	Arrowroot, cornstarch, lotus root, or amaranth starch
Potato flour	Almond flour
Xanthan gum	Guar gum (use 50% more)

Flour Blends: Mixes versus Individual Ingredients

Even though you can buy an increasing number of ready-made food items or mixes, the fact remains that 1) you can't buy everything, 2) you may not be able to afford lots of ready-made foods *or* 3) you really prefer to make your own food.

Since we can't buy all of our foods ready-made, many of you already know that wheat flour can't be replaced with one single flour. Instead, it takes a blend of flours carefully selected for their unique properties. Measuring all those flours is a bit more time consuming. Is there an easier way?

I've pondered the issue of pre-mixed flour blends (several flours blended to measure as one flour) for some time now. Yet, for every customer who wishes I would use flour blends in my books (rather than individually listed ingredients), there are those who are glad I don't because their food sensitivities don't allow the inflexibility of ready-made blends.

Furthermore, I know that certain dishes are better when made with varying amounts of the typical gluten-free flours—e.g., rice flour, potato starch, and tapioca flour. For example, chewier foods like cookies or bars require more tapioca flour than delicate items such as cakes. Therefore, it makes sense to tailor the flour blend to suit the dish rather than use the same blend for everything.

Nonetheless, I am an extremely practical person and—like you—need to minimize my time in the kitchen. For some time now, I have experimented with different blends, using a wide variety of flours. And I've become quite fond of the convenience of using a flour blend rather than always measuring 3 or 4 flours per recipe.

At the same time, I haven't forgotten that some of you can't eat legumes (which rules out the bean flours), some of you don't like rice flour, or some of you are allergic to nut flours. And, I haven't forgotten that some dishes are better made with certain kinds of flour than others.

The goal of this book is to streamline the baking process as much as possible, so I've developed a gluten-free flour blend that works well with every baked item in this book. This way, you can mix up a large batch and store it on your pantry shelf or in your refrigerator and it will be ready the next time you bake.

The blend is also versatile so you can vary the flours within the blend to suit your own personal needs. Here it is:

Carol's Gluten-Free Flour Blend

1 ½ cups sorghum flour	1 cup tapioca flour
1 ½ cups potato starch or cornstarch	½ cup corn flour or almond flour or
Makes 4.5 cups	bean flour or chestnut flour

These ingredients are readily available at your health food store or possibly your grocery store, but if they're new to you—read on. To order, check Mail-Order Sources in the Appendix.

Sorghum: Sorghum flour has been around for ages, but is finally receiving attention as a nutritious alternative to wheat. Find it at health food stores by Authentic Foods, Bob's Red Mill, and Ener-G Foods. Or, order it direct from a grower at www.twinvalleymills.com.

Corn flour: Corn flour is not the same as cornstarch. It is the whole corn kernel ground into flour rather than just the starch. You can buy it at health food stores, some grocery stores, and certain mail-order companies and on-line vendors. You can also buy yellow or white cornmeal (available at any grocery store) and grind the meal into a fine consistency with your small coffee or spice grinder. Both the yellow and white cornmeal work well, but baked goods made with the white corn flour will be somewhat lighter in color and may not brown as deeply as yellow corn flour. Be sure to choose a gluten-free brand of cornmeal.

Almond flour: Almond flour is available at www.bobsredmill.com. You can also grind your own almond flour from blanched almond slivers, using your small coffee grinder. It has a high fat content, so refrigerate and use it within two months. Be sure to grind it as finely as possible for best texture in baking. If you use almond meal it will add important fiber to your diet, but beware that if you grind whole almonds the almond skins will lend a brown tint to baked goods.

Almond flour and almond meal should be refrigerated so you'll need to refrigerate the *entire* flour blend. Bring to room temperature before using.

Potato starch: Potato starch (not potato flour) and tapioca flour (sometimes called tapioca starch) is an old standbys for us. Cornstarch can replace potato starch, if necessary. Both lend a necessary lightness to baked goods.

Tapioca flour: Sometimes called tapioca starch, it lightens baked goods while providing a nice "chew" and crustiness to the exterior of the baked goods.

Bean Flour: If corn or almond flour doesn't suit your tastes—or if you want a change—try using bean flour. This could be white bean flour from Bob's Red Mill or a blend of garbanzo/fava bean flour from the same company, or from Authentic Foods or Ener-G Foods. Bean flours, like corn flour and almond flour, add protein and fiber to the diet and nicely complement sorghum flour.

Chestnut Flour: Used frequently in Europe, this flour is available at www.dowdandrogers.com. It lends an interesting taste and texture to gluten-free baked goods. It is more expensive than the other flours we use, but you only need a small amount in the flour blend.

Which Flour Should You Use?
Almond flour has a higher fat content than corn flour and tends to make baked goods brown a lovely golden color. It is also higher in fiber. The flavor is not appreciably different whether you use almond or corn flour, but almond flour introduces a bit of texture.

Bean flour lends its own distinct "bean" flavor, but also offers a good fiber and protein content. The chestnut flour lends a nice nutty flavor and makes baked goods brown nicely. Experiment with all of these flours and see which one you like best.

Storing Your Blend
Be sure to refrigerate your flour blend if it contains nuts; they can become rancid over time. Otherwise, store it in a dark, cool place.

If refrigerated, bring the flour to room temperature before using.

I prefer the large, glass, wide-mouthed jars for storing flours because spooning and measuring from them is much easier. Others prefer plastic, re-closeable bags while some people recycle the wide-mouth canisters from Twin Valley Mills (www.twinvalleymills.com).

Nutrient Analysis of Each Flour Blend Variation

In case you're wondering, below is a comparison of the nutrient values for 1 cup of the Flour Blend with the 4 different variations (corn, almond, garbanzo/fava bean, or chestnut).

Nutrient Values of Flour Blend Variations

	Corn	Almond	Bean	Chestnut
Calories	392	391	378	369
Fat	1g	3g	1g	1g
Protein	4g	7g	5g	3g
Carbohydrates	92g	85g	88g	87g
Sodium	3mg	3mg	2mg	3mg
Cholesterol	0mg	0mg	0mg	0mg
Fiber	3g	2g	2g	2g

Source: Food Processor by ESHA Research

Now, What Does That Ingredient Do?

I'm often asked about the role of different ingredients in baking. Here is a brief explanation of what the various ingredients contribute to successful gluten-free baking.

- Cornstarch "smooths" the crust.
- Potato flour adds "chewiness" (1 teaspoon per cup of flour).
- Potato starch "lightens" dough by making it airier.
- Tapioca flour helps browning and makes a crispier crust.
- Dairy products "smooth" the crust and provide protein.
- Protein of any kind (milk, milk powder, nuts, or eggs) feeds the yeast.
- Soy lecithin makes a finer texture by acting as an emulsifier (it binds oil and water together).
- Xanthan gum prevents crumbling, as does guar gum. However, guar gum makes a slightly smoother crust on baked goods.
- Eggs "leaven" baked goods (helps them rise) and are binders.
- The acid in vinegar and lemon juice boosts the leavening action of yeast.

Culinary Terms

For some of us, being diagnosed as gluten intolerant means spending more time in the familiarity of our own kitchens. For others, it is a whole new adventure in a kitchen we hardly know and where many culinary terms might as well be in a foreign language. Here's some help with those bewildering terms.

Blend: Thoroughly combine two or more ingredients.

Boil: Heat until bubbles rise continuously and break the surface.

Chill: Refrigerate food until cold.

Combine: Stir ingredients together until thoroughly blended.

Cream: Mix fat and sugar together until soft and smooth.

Dredge: Coat or cover food lightly with flour or sugar.

Fold: Combine ingredients lightly with two motions: the first motion cuts vertically through mixture with a spatula; the second motion slides the spatula across the bottom of the bowl and up the side of the bowl. Gently repeat these motions until ingredients are blended.

Melt: Heat to a liquid state.

Mix: Combine two or more ingredients until evenly distributed.

Preheat: Heat to a desired temperature.

Puree: Blend in blender or food processor to smooth consistency.

Room temperature: Usually 75 to 80°F.

Sauté: Cook and stir in small bit of oil over high heat.

Simmer: Cook slowly in liquid at just below boiling point.

Sift: Shake in sifter to mix together and incorporate air.

Whisk: Beat with wire whisk until blended and smooth. For additional help see *Cookwise* by Shirley O. Corriher (William Morrow, 1997).

The Gluten-Free Pantry

Stocking the gluten-free pantry is similar to keeping any pantry—but we use different ingredients in *our* pantry. Here's what a well-stocked gluten-free pantry should contain. Add to it as necessary.

Ingredient	Role
Flours: Sorghum, rice, garbanzo/fava bean, corn flour, white bean, potato starch, cornstarch, tapioca, arrowroot, almond, chestnut, and sweet rice.	Create custom blends for baking; thickens sauces, gravies, and puddings.
Xanthan gum; guar gum	Prevent crumbling in baked goods; thicken sauces and salad dressings.
Gelatin Powder (unflavored)	Adds moisture and protein to baked goods; binds ingredients.
Yeast	Leavens baked goods.
Baking powder; baking soda, cream of tartar	Leavens baked goods
Dry milk powder	Adds protein; improves texture of bread. (not Carnation)
Pasta in all shapes/sizes	Use in casseroles, pasta dishes.
Parchment paper	Prevents sticking; promotes even browning
Vinegar	Makes milk into buttermilk; food for yeast.
Butter, shortening, margarine, cooking oil	Adds fat to baked goods; grease baking pans.
Plastic wrap, foil, waxed paper, paper towels	Covers food; aids in handling and shaping dough and batter.

 Carol's Tip: Replace ¼ cup of Carol's Sorghum Flour blend with flour made from quinoa, amaranth, teff, or Montina (Indian rice grass) to add flavor, fiber, and texture to baked goods. Lotus root starch and amaranth starch are good substitutes for potato starch or cornstarch

Appliances

Unless you plan to eat out for the rest of your life—or exist on ready-made foods from the supermarket or delicatessen—you'll need certain appliances for cooking in your own kitchen.

So…which appliances do you need? Aside from the necessary large appliances such as a stovetop, oven, dishwasher, and refrigerator—what is the absolute minimum for success? I think the most indispensable small appliances are: heavy-duty stand mixer, hand-held portable mixer, food processor, and bread machine (if you don't bake bread in a conventional oven).

Electric Mixers

If you bake bread, large batches of cookies, or quick breads, a heavy-duty stand mixer is a must. What is a "stand" mixer? Unlike a small portable mixer that you hold in your hand while mixing, a stand mixer sits on the countertop on its own base. It's much, much heavier (possibly weighing up to 13 pounds) and can handle heavy bread dough or large baking tasks. A lighter weight portable mixer may not be powerful enough to handle this dough or the dough may annoyingly creep up the beater shafts.

My stand mixer is a KitchenAid Ultra Power with a 4.5 quart capacity bowl. It is perfect for all of my large mixing jobs. By the way, use the regular beaters when mixing bread dough, not the dough hooks.

You will also need a small portable mixer for those quick, small mixing tasks such as whipping egg whites for meringues or making quick breads or cakes. I use a lightweight Hamilton Beach portable mixer that costs about $15 to $25; it's perfect for those jobs.

Food Processors

Many people confuse food processors with blenders or small food choppers. A blender is good for pureeing, grating, or crushing, but—unlike a food processor—it cannot mix bread or cookie dough, blend piecrust, grate hard cheese, grind meat, or slice and shred vegetables. Food processors are especially good for blending gluten-free dough because they distribute liquid ingredients more thoroughly and more quickly than other methods—producing silkier, more resilient, and moister baked items.

You don't need an expensive version. I wrote my first two cookbooks using an inexpensive, $30 food processor. After daily use for many years, it wore out. I then bought a KitchenAid with a 7 cup capacity for under $100 at a discount store. It's much heavier, has only three switches (on/off/pulse), and performs beautifully.

If you're looking for brand recommendations, you can't go wrong with KitchenAid, Cuisinart, Black & Decker, or Hamilton Beach but there may be other brands that work as well.

Bread Machines

If you're not a baker, then a bread machine may be your salvation because it eliminates the guesswork. You don't have to monitor the rising and baking times as you do when making bread by hand.

However, there are some downsides to bread machines. Most are pre-programmed for gluten breads which require two risings. Gluten-free bread requires only one rise, so that second rise adds unnecessary time. One way around this is to buy a machine that allows you to program the cycles. However, these machines are more expensive.

In addition, the paddles make indentations on the underside of the loaf, and the pan or bucket might be a cylinder rather than a loaf shape. Bread baked in a bread machine rarely produces a "dome" or nicely rounded top (as it does with an oven-baked loaf).

Finally, we can't take advantage of some of the bread machine's time saving aspects such as programming our breads to bake overnight. Most of our breads require eggs which should not sit overnight in the machine.

Nonetheless, despite all these disadvantages, some people prefer bread machines. Here are some tips for that perfect loaf.

Choosing Your Bread Machine

With the constant changes in appliances, some of this information may be out of date by the time you read this book. Generally speaking, the brands most commonly used are Regal Kitchen Pro, Welbilt (now owned by Salton), Breadman Ultimate, and Zojirushi V20. This doesn't mean that other brands won't make good bread. However, I notice that when people are having problems with bread machines, it's less likely with the brands mentioned above.

Features to consider

Bucket or Pan Size: Some people prefer to bake smaller loaves (e.g., 1 pound) and have fresh bread frequently by baking more often. Others prefer to bake larger loaves (1 ½ to 2 pounds) because they have larger families or like to bake large quantities for freezing. I personally think that the smaller, 1 pound loaves turn out better than the larger 2 pound loaves.

Cycles: Ideally, your bread machine has an option for one rise perhaps called a short or rapid cycle. However, most of our bread machines have two cycles. Don't despair. There are ways to handle this (see How to Use a Bread Machine below).

Paddles: Generally, larger paddles are better. However, there are ways to handle this, too. (see How to Use Your Bread Machine below.)

Be sure to use the right size recipe for your machine. Too many novice cooks unknowingly use a 1 ½ to 2 pound recipe in a 1 pound bread machine. The dough overflows, causing a mess.

Shape: Some machines produce loaves that are cylindrical (round); others are square. Still others are loaf shaped. I've found all three acceptable. However, buy the loaf shape if your family is committed to conventional loaf-shaped sandwiches.

Price: The price of bread machines has dropped considerably since I purchased my first one in 1994. You can get a good machine for well under $100. The popular Zojirushi is programmable and costs about $170-$200, depending on where you buy it.

How to Use Your Bread Machine

We gluten-free bakers are a creative bunch, so here are some tricks of the trade from my own experiences as well as tips from many of you.

Preparing and Adding Ingredients
• Measure carefully, using standard cups and spoons (no teaspoons from the silverware drawer).

• Have ingredients at room temperature.

• Blend liquid ingredients together thoroughly, using a wire whisk or electric mixer (egg membranes must be completely broken up).

• Follow your machine instructions about the order of adding ingredients (liquids first, dry ingredients next, or vice versa).

• Even though the bucket/pan is nonstick, lightly grease or use some cooking spray to assure quick release and easy cleaning.

Selecting the Cycle/Program/Setting
• Some machines have settings for the crust color, such as light or medium. You may have to make bread twice—the same recipe on two different settings—to see which works best. I rarely use the dark setting.

• If you'd rather not have your bread go through two rises (and you can't program your machine), determine when the second rise begins from your machine's instruction booklet. Set a timer so you can be ready when the second rise starts. For example, in the Welbilt example below, I would set the time for 50 minutes because that's when the rise begins.

• About 10 minutes before the 50 minutes is up, thoroughly mix all the bread ingredients together. Put the dough into the bucket/pan and when the timer rings, listen for the bread machine beep (or watch the LCD or LED window display) and insert the bucket/pan at the right moment.

• If you use the above method, you don't need the paddle and therefore, you won't have the paddle marks in your loaf.

• To program your machine, adapt the cycle information below. It's from my 1 pound Welbilt and a modification of recommendations from Red Star Yeast. The third column is for a Zojirushi BBC-V20 on Home Made setting. You may have to modify your machine cycle, but at least you have a reference point now.

Cycles for Bread Machines

Welbilt (1 lb)	Red Star Yeast	Zojirushi (1 lb)
Warm 20 minutes*	Warm 20 minutes*	Preheat 20 minutes*
Knead 10 minutes	Knead 20 minutes	Knead 25 minutes
Rest 5 minutes		
Knead 15 minutes		
First rise: 25 minutes	First rise: None.	First rise: None
Second rise: 54 minutes	Second rise: 70 minutes	Second rise: 35 minutes
Bake 40 minutes	Bake 60 minutes	Bake 60 minutes
Total: 2 hr., 49 minutes	Total: 2 hr. 50 minutes	Total: 2 hr. 20 minutes

*Some machines don't do this

• Another way to eliminate the second rise is available on my Welbilt ABMY2K2 Baker's Select machine. After the first rise, stop the machine and cancel the cycle by pressing the STOP key until it beeps. Set the machine to the BAKE setting and press the START key. (Of course, you have to be there to do this—thus reducing the convenience of bread machines in the first place.)

• Rising time can vary considerably, depending on the altitude, humidity, and type of flours being used. So, you may need to alter these rising times to suit your particular situation.

During Mixing and Baking
• Use a spatula to scrape down the bucket sides during first mixing.

• Listen for beeps that signal when to add mix-ins (raisins, nuts).

• Don't raise the lid if your machine says not to—it cancels the cycle entirely. If this happens, quickly transfer dough to greased pan and finish the rise. Then bake in a conventional oven at 375°F.

• Unless you're instructed otherwise, choose a normal or medium setting. One of the common problems is underbaking, rather than overbaking the bread. So, don't be afraid to extend the baking time if you can program the cycles.

• Watch the dough through the window the first few times you use a bread machine. Learn to recognize the right appearance and texture at each stage. Take notes if you adjust the recipe (like adding more flour or more liquid) so you know what to do next time.

• Many gluten-free bakers mistakenly think that a very soft bread dough doesn't look right. Actually, gluten-free bread dough should be fairly soft and drop gracefully in globs from a spatula, rather than you having to pry the dough from the spatula.

• Once you've learned how the dough should look, you can modify it by adding more water or flour during the mixing stage. Generally, there should be soft lines on the top of the dough indicating the path of the paddles, if used.

After Baking
• Some machines will keep your bread warm after baking. Others do not. For best results, don't leave bread in the machine too long or moisture build-up softens the crust.

• If the crust isn't crisp enough or the bread seems underdone, transfer the loaf to a baking sheet and bake another 10 to 15 minutes in a preheated conventional oven or until desired doneness.

• To test for doneness, insert an instant-read thermometer in the middle or thickest part of the loaf. It should read 200°F to 205°F.

• Use the manufacturer's toll-free Customer Service department to let them know if you have problems or questions. Sometimes the bread machines are defective.

• One final thought. Buying all these appliances may seem expensive, but you'll use them for a long, long time. So, you're really investing in your health and your future. Would you rather spend more money on physician's visits, prescription drugs, and lost productivity at work—or spend a little more money on appliances to make your kitchen time as productive as possible and have good, safe food?

Also, by the time you read this some of these brands may have become obsolete of the models may have changed.

Troubleshooting the Problem Loaf

Sometimes, things don't go as planned when we're baking bread in a bread machine. Below are some common problems and their recommended solutions.

Problem	Solution for the Next Time You Bake
Cratered top	Too much liquid. Add flour, 1 tablespoon at a time.
Mushroom top	Too much yeast. Reduce by ½ teaspoon
Gnarly, rough top	Not enough liquid. Add liquid, 1 Tablespoon at a time. Another Tablespoon of sugar may help or using more cornstarch in the flour blend.
Unbaked inside	Adjust cycle to bake longer or finish baking in a conventional oven or bake loaves in several smaller pans.

Now, if you're determined to bake bread the old-fashioned way, turn to the next chapter for great tips on making bread the way we did it before bread machines came along.

ᘓ• Bread •ᘓ
The Staff of Life

Basic Primer on Baking Bread 54

Savory Breads

Bagels 80-82	*French Bread 75*
Basic Bread 56	*Hamburger Buns 76*
Breadsticks 71	*Herb Buns 76*
Bread Crumbs 58	*High-Fiber Bread 65*
Cheese Bread Balls 72	*Hot Dog Buns 76*
Cheese Bread Sandwich Buns 72	*Montina Bread 61*
Corn Bread 73	*Muffaletta (Sandwiches) 74*
"Cracked Wheat" Bread 59	*Popovers 77*
Croutons 58	*Potato Bread 78*
Dinner Rolls 58	*Pumpernickel Bread 69*
Fennel Bread 63	*Yorkshire Pudding 77*
Focaccia (Italian flatbread) 74	

Sweet Breads

Cinnamon Rolls 58	*Raisin Bread 67*

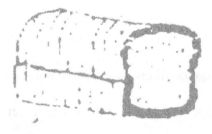

For Breakfast breads, see page 79

For more delicious breads see:
Wheat-Free Recipes & Menus: Delicious, Healthful Eating for People with Food Sensitivities by Carol Fenster, Ph.D.
Cooking Free; 200 Flavorful Recipes for People with Food Allergies & Multiple Food Sensitivities by Carol Fenster, Ph.D.
Gluten-Free Quick & Easy--From Prep to Plate without the Fuss by Carol Fenster, Ph.D.
1,000 Gluten-Free Recipes by Carol Fenster, Ph.D.

ভ্র• A Basic Primer on Baking Bread •ড়

If you're determined to bake bread the old-fashioned way—in a conventional oven—then this primer should help assure success each and every time.

READY, SET . . . Planning Ahead for Success!
1. Have ingredients at room temperature; check yeast expiration.

2. Have all ingredients measured and on one side of workspace before beginning. As you add each ingredient, place on opposite side of workspace.

3. Use standard measuring utensils; measure correctly
     a. Run a whisk through the flour a few times
     b. Spoon flour lightly into measuring cup (don't pack)
     c. Level flour with straight edge of knife

4. Use the proper type and size of pan. Nonstick pans (gray, not black) conduct heat and brown the bread better than glass or shiny aluminum. Generously grease the pan (and dust with flour, if desired). An 8 x 4-inch pan is used for 1 pound loaves; a 9 x 5-inch pan is used for 1 ½ pound loaves. Small pans work better than large pans because the heated air can reach the center of the loaf more easily.

5. Use your favorite recipe. To boost fiber and nutrition, add rice bran or rice polish, sorghum grits, hemp seed, flaxmeal, potato flour, and almond or pecan meal. Start slowly; add 1 to 2 tablespoons per loaf—increase to ¼ cup later as your body adjusts to the fiber.

6. Check oven temperature with oven thermometer.

GO! . . Mixing It Up!
1. Dissolve yeast in warm liquid (110°F). Filtered water works better than tap water. Use heavy-duty mixer with regular beaters.

2. Beat all ingredients one minute to incorporate air and "set" xanthan gum.

3. Dough should fall gracefully off beaters in "globs," rather than cling firmly or drip like water. It should look like "fluffy frosting" or stiff cake batter. If you

have to pry the dough from the beater, it's too stiff and needs more liquid. If it runs off the batter in a thin stream, it's too wet and needs more flour.

4. Smooth dough in pan with wet spatula for smoother crust and even rising.

5. Cover with foil tent, let rise in warm place (75 to 80°F). Place in an enclosed area (e.g., oven or microwave) to avoid drafts.

6. Dough should be no higher than top of pan. "Oven-spring" will cause dough to rise even higher while baking.

BAKING . . . The Heat Is On!
1. Preheat oven. Bake for the specified amount of time. Don't under-bake—this is one of the chief causes of fallen bread!

2. For a crisper crust in French bread and flat breads such as focaccia, place risen bread in *cold* oven and then turn oven on to desired heat. This also works especially well for bagels and breadsticks, but will not work with full-size loaves—or if your oven preheats with the broiler only.

3. Cover with foil after 10 minutes to avoid over-browning. Don't open the door again.

4. A properly baked loaf sounds crisp or hard when tapped with fingernail. An internal temperature of 200 to 205°F indicates "done".

5. I prefer smaller baking pans (8 x 4-inch or several 5 x 3-inch), or French loaves or baguettes, because the dough bakes more quickly and evenly. Use parchment paper to prevent leakage if you use perforated pans (such as a pizza pan).

6. After baking, cool in pan for 5 minutes. Then cool on wire rack.

7. When thoroughly cooled, slice with serrated or electric knife. Store bread in a freezer or refrigerator.

8. Most bread can benefit from a gentle re-warming in the microwave—especially when it's frozen or a few days old. Use 30 second increments at 30 to 40 percent power until the bread reaches desired state. Do not reheat bread on High power.

ভ· Basic Bread ·৪০

One easy recipe—in three different sizes.

Basic Bread Pan size	1 Pound (8 x 4-inch) Serves 10	1 ½ Pound (9 x 5-inch) Serves 15	2 Pound (Two 8 x 4-inch) Serves 20
Active dry yeast	2 ¼ teaspoons	2 ¼ teaspoons	2 ¼ teaspoons
Sugar	1 tablespoon	4 ½ teaspoons	2 tablespoons
Water (110°F)	1 cup	1 ½ cups	2 cups
Flour Blend (page 41)	1 ½ cups	2 ¼ cups	3 cups
Potato starch	½ cup	½ cup	¾ cup
Dry milk powder- (not Carnation) (cow, rice, soy)	¼ cup	⅓ cup	½ cup
Xanthan gum	1 ½ teaspoons	2 teaspoons	3 teaspoons
Guar gum	1 teaspoon	1 teaspoon	1 teaspoon
Salt	¾ teaspoon	1 teaspoon	1 ¼ teaspoons
Soy lecithin	¼ teaspoon	½ teaspoon	1 teaspoon
Large eggs	1 large egg	2 large eggs	2 large eggs
Butter/canola oil	1 tablespoon	1 ½ tablespoons	2 tablespoons
Cider vinegar	½ teaspoon	½ teaspoon	1 teaspoon

Hand Method

1. Combine dry yeast, 2 teaspoons of the sugar, and warm water. Set aside to let yeast foam, about 5 minutes.

2. In bowl of heavy-duty stand mixer (regular beaters, not dough hooks), combine yeast-mixture with remaining ingredients (including remaining sugar).

3. Blend on medium speed for 1 minute, scraping down sides with spatula if necessary.

4. Place dough in greased pan(s). Cover lightly with foil and let rise at room temperature (75 to 80º) until dough is level with top of pan. Rising time will vary from 45 to 60+ minutes, depending on altitude and humidity.

5. Preheat oven to 375ºF. With sharp knife, make three diagonal slashes ⅛-inch deep in loaf so steam can escape during baking.

6. Bake 55 to 65 minutes, or until nicely browned and internal temperature is 205°F on an instant-read thermometer. Do not underbake. Cover with foil tent after 20 minutes of baking to reduce overbrowning.

Bread Machine
Follow bread machine instructions, making sure machine is appropriate size for recipe. With my machine, I whisk dry ingredients together (including yeast) and add to pan. Then, I whisk liquid ingredients together (water at room temperature) and pour carefully over dry ingredients. Set controls and bake. I use "Normal" setting.

Calories 185; Fat 2g; Protein 3g; Carbohydrates 40g; Sodium 192mg; Cholesterol 21mg; Fiber <1g

---

 Carol's Tip: See Bread 101—a step-by-step guide for baking gluten-free bread by hand at www.glutenfree101.com. Click on Recipes, then Bread Recipes, then Bread 101.

ભ⁘ Look What You Can Do with a Basic Bread Recipe •ৼ⊃

Dinner Rolls (pull-apart style): To the 1 pound Basic Bread recipe on page 56, add ¾ cup cornstarch and ¼ teaspoon salt. Mix as directed. Use 1 ½-inch spring-action ice cream scoop to drop 18 balls of dough into greased 11 x 7-inch pan or 9 x 9-inch nonstick pan. Cover loosely and let rise in warm place (75 to 80°F) until level with top of pan. Bake 25 minutes in preheated 375°F oven or until lightly browned. Cool on wire rack. Serves 18 (one roll each).

Cinnamon Rolls: To the 1 pound Basic Bread recipe on page 56 add ½ cup cornstarch and 2 tablespoons sugar to dry ingredients. Grease a 12-cup standard muffin pan. Combine 1 cup brown sugar, 1 teaspoon cinnamon, and ¼ cup finely chopped pecans. Set aside.

Place ¼ of dough on surface liberally dusted with rice flour; generously dust dough with rice flour. Roll to ½-inch thickness. Sprinkle with ¼ of sugar-cinnamon-pecan mixture. Cut into three strips. Roll up each strip and place in muffin tin, cut side down. Repeat with remaining dough. Bake 25 to 30 minutes or until tops are nicely browned. Cool. Top with powdered sugar frosting, if desired. Makes 12 rolls.

Calories 215; Fat 4g; Protein 2g; Carbohydrates45g; Sodium 167mg; Cholesterol 21mg; Fiber 1g

Here's What to Do with Leftover Gluten-Free Bread

Bread Crumbs: In food processor, combine 4 cups bread torn in small pieces, 1 teaspoon onion powder, and 4 teaspoons Italian herb seasoning. Pulse on/off until crumbs reach desired consistency. Makes 2 cups. Store tightly covered, in refrigerator, for up to 2 weeks.

Croutons: Slice bread in ½-inch slices; cut off crusts. Cut in ½-inch cubes. Toast in 325°F oven. Add Italian seasoning to taste.

⚘ "Cracked Wheat" Bread ⚘

This is bread the way I used to eat it. Hearty, with a palate-satisfying texture. I baked this bread every weekend and as soon as it came out of the oven, I sliced off the heel and slathered it with butter. Along with a cup of freshly brewed coffee, I was in heaven.

Basic Bread Pan size	**1 Pound** (8 x 4-inch) *Serves 10*	**1 ½ Pound** (9 x 5-inch) *Serves 15*	**2 Pound** (Two 8 x 4-inch) *Serves 20*
Active dry yeast	2 ¼ teaspoons	2 ¼ teaspoons	2 ¼ teaspoons
Sugar	1 tablespoon	4 ½ teaspoons	2 tablespoons
Water (110ºF)	1 cup	1 ½ cups	2 cups
Flour Blend (page 41)	1 ½ cups	2 ¼ cups	3 cups
Potato starch	½ cup	½ cup	¾ cup
Dry milk powder (not Carnation) (cow, rice, soy)	¼ cup	⅓ cup	½ cup
Xanthan gum	1 ½ teaspoons	2 teaspoons	3 teaspoons
Guar gum	1 teaspoon	1 teaspoon	1 teaspoon
Salt	¾ teaspoon	1 teaspoon	1 ¼ teaspoons
Soy lecithin	¼ teaspoon	½ teaspoon	1 teaspoon
Large eggs	1 large egg	2 large eggs	2 large eggs
Butter/canola oil	1 tablespoon	1 ½ tablespoons	2 tablespoons
Cider vinegar	½ teaspoon	½ teaspoon	1 teaspoon
Whole wehani rice or brown rice	¼ cup	⅓ cup	½ cup

Hand Method

1. Combine dry yeast, 2 teaspoons of the sugar, and warm water. Set aside to let yeast foam, about 5 minutes.

2. Pulverize rice in small coffee grinder until "cracked" then place in bowl of heavy-duty stand mixer (regular beaters, not dough hooks), along with yeast-mixture and remaining ingredients (including remaining sugar).

3. Blend on medium speed for 1 minute, scraping down sides with spatula if necessary.

4. Place dough in greased pan(s). Cover lightly with foil and let rise at room temperature (75 to 80°F) until dough is level with top of pan. (Rising time will vary from 45 to 60+ minutes or more, depending on altitude and humidity.)

5. Preheat oven to 375°F. With a sharp knife, make three diagonal slashes ⅛-inch deep in loaf so steam can escape during baking.

6. Bake 55 to 65 minutes, or until nicely browned and internal temperature is 205°F on an instant-read thermometer. Do not underbake. Cover with foil tent after 20 minutes of baking to reduce over-browning.

Bread Machine

Follow bread machine instructions, making sure machine is appropriate size for recipe. With my machine, I whisk dry ingredients together (including yeast) and add to pan. Then, I whisk liquid ingredients together (water at room temperature) and pour carefully over dry ingredients. Set controls and bake. I use "Normal" setting.

Calories 200; Fat 2g; Protein 3g; Carbohydrates 44g; Sodium 191mg; Cholesterol 21mg; Fiber <1g

↝• Montina Bread •↜

Montina is the name given to Indian ricegrass, grown in the Northwest. It resembles whole wheat flakes and produces hearty, earthy bread that makes great sandwiches.

Basic Bread Pan size	**1 Pound** (8 x 4-inch) Serves 10	**1 ½ Pound** (9 x 5-inch) Serves 15	**2 Pound** (Two 8 x 4-inch) Serves 20
Active dry yeast	2 ¼ teaspoons	2 ¼ teaspoons	2 ¼ teaspoons
Sugar	1 tablespoon	4 ½ teaspoons	2 tablespoons
Water (110ºF)	1 cup	1 ½ cups	2 cups
Flour Blend (page 41)	1 ¼ cups	2 cups	2 ¼ cups
Montina Pure Supplement	¼ cup	½ cup	¾ cup
Potato starch	½ cup	½ cup	¾ cup
Dry milk powder (not Carnation) (cow, rice, soy)	¼ cup	⅓ cup	½ cup
Xanthan gum	1 ½ teaspoons	2 teaspoons	3 teaspoons
Guar gum	1 teaspoon	1 teaspoon	1 teaspoon
Salt	¾ teaspoon	1 teaspoon	1 ¼ teaspoons
Soy lecithin	¼ teaspoon	½ teaspoon	1 teaspoon
Large eggs	1 large egg	2 large eggs	2 large eggs
Butter/canola oil	1 tablespoon	1 ½ tablespoons	2 tablespoons
Cider vinegar	½ teaspoon	½ teaspoon	1 teaspoon

Hand Method

1. Combine dry yeast, 2 teaspoons of the sugar, and warm water. Set aside to let yeast foam, about 5 minutes.

2. In bowl of heavy-duty stand mixer (regular beaters, not dough hooks), combine yeast-mixture with remaining ingredients (including remaining sugar).

3. Blend on medium speed for 1 minute, scraping down sides with spatula if necessary.

4. Place dough in greased pan(s). Cover lightly with foil and let rise at room temperature (75 to 80°F) until dough is level with top of pan. (Rising time will vary from 45 to 60+ minutes, depending on altitude and humidity.)

5. Preheat oven to 375°F. With a sharp knife, make three diagonal slashes ⅛-inch deep in loaf so steam can escape during baking.

6. Bake 55 to 65 minutes, or until nicely browned and internal temperature is 205°F on an instant-read thermometer. Do not underbake. Cover with foil tent after 20 minutes of baking to reduce overbrowning.

Bread Machine

Follow bread machine instructions, making sure machine is appropriate size for recipe. With my machine, I whisk dry ingredients together (including yeast) and add to pan. Then, I whisk liquid ingredients together (water at room temperature) and pour carefully over dry ingredients. Set controls and bake. I use "Normal" setting.

Calories 195; Fat 2g; Protein 3g; Carbohydrates 41g; Sodium 188mg; Cholesterol 21mg; Fiber 1g

ℭℨ• Fennel Bread •℘

Fennel seed adds a savory taste to plain bread that will make your guests ask for more.

Basic Bread Pan size	1 Pound (8 x 4-inch) *Serves 10*	1 ½ Pound (9 x 5-inch) *Serves 15*	2 Pound (Two 8 x 4-inch) *Serves 20*
Active dry yeast	2 ¼ teaspoons	2 ¼ teaspoons	2 ¼ teaspoons
Sugar	1 tablespoon	4 ½ teaspoons	2 tablespoons
Water (110°F)	1 cup	1 ½ cups	2 cups
Flour Blend (page 41)	1 ½ cups	2 ¼ cups	3 cups
Potato starch	½ cup	½ cup	¾ cup
Dry milk powder (not Carnation) (cow, rice, soy)	¼ cup	⅓ cup	½ cup
Xanthan gum	1 ½ teaspoons	2 teaspoons	3 teaspoons
Guar gum	1 teaspoon	1 teaspoon	1 teaspoon
Salt	¾ teaspoon	1 teaspoon	1 ¼ teaspoons
Soy lecithin	¼ teaspoon	½ teaspoon	1 teaspoon
Large eggs	1 large egg	2 large eggs	2 large eggs
Butter/canola oil	1 tablespoon	1 ½ tablespoons	2 tablespoons
Cider vinegar	½ teaspoon	½ teaspoon	1 teaspoon
Fennel seeds	1 tablespoon	1 ½ tablespoons	2 tablespoons
Molasses	1 tablespoon	1 ½ tablespoons	2 tablespoons

Hand Method

1. Combine dry yeast, 2 teaspoons of the sugar, and warm water. Set aside to let yeast foam, about 5 minutes.

2. In bowl of heavy-duty stand mixer (regular beaters, not dough hooks), combine yeast-mixture with remaining ingredients (including remaining sugar).

3. Blend on medium speed for 1 minute, scraping down sides with spatula if necessary.

4. Place dough in greased pan(s). Cover lightly with foil and let rise at room temperature (75 to 80°F) until dough is level with top of pan. (Rising time will vary from 45 to 60+ minutes, depending on altitude and humidity.)

5. Preheat oven to 375°F. With a sharp knife, make three diagonal slashes ⅛-inch deep in loaf so steam can escape during baking.

6. Bake 55 to 65 minutes, or until nicely browned and internal temperature is 205°F on an instant-read thermometer. Do not underbake. Cover with foil tent after 20 minutes of baking to reduce over-browning.

Bread Machine

Follow bread machine instructions, making sure machine is appropriate size for recipe. With my machine, I whisk dry ingredients together (including yeast) and add to pan. Then, I whisk liquid ingredients together (water at room temperature) and pour carefully over dry ingredients. Set controls and bake. I use "Normal" setting.

Calories 210; Fat 2.5g; Protein 3g; Carbohydrates 46g; Sodium 192mg; Cholesterol 21mg; Fiber <1g

ভ. High-Fiber Bread ·৪০

The addition of nutritious seeds and grains makes this bread a powerhouse of fiber.

Basic Bread Pan size	1 Pound (8 x 4-inch) Serves 10	1 ½ Pound (9 x 5-inch) Serves 15	2 Pound (Two 8 x 4-inch) Serves 20
Active dry yeast	2 ¼ teaspoons	2 ¼ teaspoons	2 ¼ teaspoons
Sugar	1 tablespoon	4 ½ teaspoons	2 tablespoons
Water (110°F)	1 cup	1 ½ cups	2 cups
Flour Blend (page 41)	1 ½ cups	2 ¼ cups	3 cups
Potato starch	½ cup	½ cup	¾ cup
Dry milk powder (not Carnation) (cow, rice, soy)	¼ cup	⅓ cup	½ cup
Xanthan gum	1 ½ teaspoons	2 teaspoons	3 teaspoons
Guar gum	1 teaspoon	1 teaspoon	1 teaspoon
Salt	¾ teaspoon	1 teaspoon	1 ¼ teaspoons
Soy lecithin	¼ teaspoon	½ teaspoon	1 teaspoon
Large eggs	1 large egg	2 large eggs	2 large eggs
Butter/canola oil	1 tablespoon	1 ½ tablespoons	2 tablespoons
Cider vinegar	½ teaspoon	½ teaspoon	1 teaspoon
Rice bran or polish	½ cup	¾ cup	1 cup
Flax meal	2 teaspoons	1 tablespoon	1 tablespoon

Hand Method

1. Combine dry yeast, 2 teaspoons of the sugar, and warm water. Set aside to let yeast foam, about 5 minutes.

2. In bowl of heavy-duty stand mixer (regular beaters, not dough hooks), combine yeast-mixture with remaining ingredients (including remaining sugar).

3. Blend on medium speed for 1 minute, scraping down sides with spatula if necessary.

4. Place dough in greased pan(s). Cover lightly with foil and let rise at room temperature (75 to 80°F) until dough is level with top of pan. (Rising time will vary from 45 to 60+ minutes, depending on altitude and humidity.)

5. Preheat oven to 375°F. With a sharp knife, make three diagonal slashes ⅛-inch deep in loaf so steam can escape during baking.

6. Bake 55 to 65 minutes, or until nicely browned and internal temperature is 205°F on an instant-read thermometer.. Do not underbake. Cover with foil tent after 20 minutes of baking to reduce overbrowning.

Bread Machine

Follow bread machine instructions, making sure machine is appropriate size for recipe. With my machine, I whisk dry ingredients together (including yeast) and add to pan. Then, I whisk liquid ingredients together (water at room temperature) and pour carefully over dry ingredients. Set controls and bake. I use "Normal" setting.

Calories 260; Fat 6g; Protein 5g; Carbohydrates 51g; Sodium 237mg; Cholesterol 39mg; Fiber 2g

ᘓᐧ Raisin Bread ᐧᘔ

This bread is great for breakfast, toasted and topped with cream cheese or apple butter.

Basic Bread Pan size	1 Pound (8 x 4-inch) *Serves 10*	1 ½ Pound (9 x 5-inch) *Serves 15*	2 Pound (Two 8 x 4-inch) *Serves 20*
Active dry yeast	2 ¼ teaspoons	2 ¼ teaspoons	2 ¼ teaspoons
Sugar	1 tablespoon	4 ½ teaspoons	2 tablespoons
Water (110°F)	1 cup	1 ½ cups	2 cups
Flour Blend (page 41)	1 ½ cups	2 ¼ cups	3 cups
Potato starch	½ cup	½ cup	¾ cup
Dry milk powder (not Carnation) (cow, rice, soy)	¼ cup	⅓ cup	½ cup
Xanthan gum	1 ½ teaspoons	2 teaspoons	3 teaspoons
Guar gum	1 teaspoon	1 teaspoon	1 teaspoon
Salt	¾ teaspoon	1 teaspoon	1 ¼ teaspoons
Soy lecithin	¼ teaspoon	½ teaspoon	1 teaspoon
Large eggs	1 large egg	2 large eggs	2 large eggs
Butter/canola oil	1 tablespoon	1 ½ tablespoons	2 tablespoons
Cider vinegar	½ teaspoon	½ teaspoon	1 teaspoon
Cinnamon	1 teaspoon	1 ½ teaspoons	2 teaspoons
Raisins (add after dough is mixed)	½ cup	¾ cup	1 cup

Hand Method

1. Combine dry yeast, 2 teaspoons of the sugar, and warm water. Set aside to let yeast foam, about 5 minutes.

2. In bowl of heavy-duty stand mixer (regular beaters, not dough hooks), combine yeast-mixture with remaining ingredients (flour through cinnamon, including remaining sugar).

3. Blend on medium speed for 1 minute, scraping down sides with spatula if necessary. Stir in raisins.

4. Place dough in greased pan(s). Cover lightly with foil and let rise at room temperature (75 to 80ºF) until dough is level with top of pan. (Rising time will vary from 45 to 60+ minutes or more, depending on altitude and humidity.)

5. Preheat oven to 375°F With a sharp knife, make three diagonal slashes ⅛-inch deep in loaf so steam can escape during baking.

6. Bake 55 to 65 minutes, or until nicely browned and internal temperature is 205°F on an instant-read thermometer. Do not underbake. Cover with foil tent after 20 minutes of baking to reduce overbrowning.

Bread Machine

Follow bread machine instructions, making sure machine is appropriate size for recipe. With my machine, I whisk dry ingredients together (including yeast) and add to pan. Then, I whisk liquid ingredients together (water at room temperature) and pour carefully over dry ingredients. Set controls and bake. I use "Normal" setting. Add the raisins as directed by your machine directions.

Calories 225; Fat 2.5g; Protein 3g; Carbohydrates 50g; Sodium 194mg; Cholesterol 21mg; Fiber 1g

 Carol's Tip: See Bread 101—a step-by-step guide for baking gluten-free bread by hand at www.glutenfree101.com. Click on Recipes, then Bread Recipes, then Bread 101.

ༀ• Pumpernickel Bread •ༀ

I use this bread for hearty sandwiches of pastrami, corned beef, or plain old tuna salad.

Basic Bread **Pan size**	**1 Pound** (8 x 4-inch) *Serves 10*	**1 ½ Pound** (9 x 5-inch) *Serves 15*	**2 Pound** (Two 8 x 4-inch) *Serves 20*
Active dry yeast	2 ¼ teaspoons	2 ¼ teaspoons	2 ¼ teaspoons
Sugar	1 tablespoon	4 ½ teaspoons	2 tablespoons
Water (110°F)	1 cup	1 ½ cups	2 cups
Flour Blend (page 41)	1 ½ cups	2 ¼ cups	3 cups
Potato starch	½ cup	½ cup	¾ cup
Dry milk powder (not Carnation) (cow, rice, soy)	¼ cup	⅓ cup	½ cup
Xanthan gum	1 ½ teaspoons	2 teaspoons	3 teaspoons
Guar gum	1 teaspoon	1 teaspoon	1 teaspoon
Salt	¾ teaspoon	1 teaspoon	1 ¼ teaspoons
Soy lecithin	¼ teaspoon	½ teaspoon	1 teaspoon
Large eggs	1 large egg	2 large eggs	2 large eggs
Butter/canola oil	1 tablespoon	1 ½ tablespoons	2 tablespoons
Cider vinegar	½ teaspoon	½ teaspoon	1 teaspoon
Brown sugar	⅓ cup	½ cup	⅔ cup
Cocoa	1 tablespoon	1 ½ tablespoons	2 tablespoons
Caraway seeds	1 tablespoon	1 ½ tablespoons	2 tablespoons
Molasses	2 teaspoons	3 teaspoons	4 teaspoons
Onion powder	½ teaspoon	¾ teaspoon	1 teaspoon
Grated orange rind	1 teaspoon	1 ½ teaspoons	2 teaspoons

Hand Method

1. Combine dry yeast, 2 teaspoons of the sugar, and warm water. Set aside to let yeast foam, about 5 minutes.

2. In bowl of heavy-duty stand mixer (regular beaters, not dough hooks), combine yeast-mixture with remaining ingredients (including remaining sugar).

3. Blend on medium speed for 1 minute, scraping down sides with spatula if necessary.

4. Place dough in greased pan(s). Cover lightly with foil and let rise at room temperature (75 to 80°) until dough is level with top of pan. (Rising time will vary from 45 to 60+ minutes, depending on altitude and humidity.)

5. Preheat oven to 375°F. With a sharp knife, make three diagonal slashes ⅛-inch deep in loaf so steam can escape during baking.

6. Bake 55 to 65 minutes, or until nicely browned and internal temperature is 205°F on an instant-read thermometer.. Do not underbake. Cover with foil tent after 20 minutes of baking to reduce overbrowning.

Bread Machine

Follow bread machine instructions, making sure machine is appropriate size for recipe. With my machine, I whisk dry ingredients together (including yeast) and add to pan. Then, I whisk liquid ingredients together (water at room temperature) and pour carefully over dry ingredients. Set controls and bake. I use "Normal" setting.

Calories 210; Fat 2.5g; Protein 3g; Carbohydrates 45g; Sodium 192mg; Cholesterol 21mg; Fiber 1g

ෲ• Breadsticks •ଆ

These breadsticks are so easy you'll make them again and again. For bigger breadsticks, increase rising time or cut a bigger hole in the plastic bag. Adjust baking time accordingly.

1 tablespoon active dry yeast	1 tablespoon olive oil
½ teaspoon sugar	2 teaspoons xanthan gum
⅔ cup warm (110°F) milk (cow, rice, soy)	1 teaspoon onion powder
½ cup Flour Blend (page 41)	1 teaspoon unflavored gelatin powder
½ cup tapioca flour	½ teaspoon salt
½ cup grated Parmesan cheese	1 teaspoon cider vinegar
(cow, rice, soy)	1 teaspoon Italian herb seasoning

1. Preheat oven to 400°F for 10 minutes; then turn off. Dissolve yeast and sugar in warm milk. Grease large baking sheet.

2. In medium mixer bowl, beat remaining ingredients (except Italian seasoning) plus yeast-water mixture on high 1 minute. Dough will be soft and sticky. (Bread machine is not recommended.)

3. Place dough in large, *heavy-duty* plastic freezer bag that has ½-inch corner cut off. (This makes a 1-inch circle.) Squeeze dough out of plastic bag onto sheet in 10 strips, each 1-inch wide by 6 inches long. For best results, hold bag of dough upright as you squeeze, rather than at an angle. Also, hold bag with seam on top, rather than at side. Spray breadsticks with cooking spray; then sprinkle with Italian herb seasoning.

4. Place in oven to rise for 20 to 30 minutes. Then, leaving breadsticks in oven, turn oven to 400°F and bake until golden brown—about 15 to 20 minutes. Rotate position of cookie sheet halfway through baking to assure even browning. Cool on wire rack. When cool, store in airtight container. Makes 10 breadsticks (1 per serving).

Calories: 90; Fat 3g; Protein 3g; Carbohydrates 12g; Sodium 232mg; Cholesterol 4mg; Fiber <1g

ೞ• Cheese Bread Balls •ಐ

These little morsels are from Brazil, where they are called Pao De Quiejo. They're quick, easy and very, very tasty. Use them as snacks, dinner rolls—or slice them in half, toast them, and use them for sandwiches. They'll be crisp on the outside, sticky on the inside.

1 ½ cups tapioca flour
1 cup milk (cow, rice, soy)
¼ cup light olive oil
1 large egg

½ cup grated Parmesan, Romano, or
   Asiago cheese (or soy or rice substitute)
¼ teaspoon salt

1. Preheat oven to 375°F. Have tapioca flour measured and ready.

2. Heat milk and oil in medium saucepan and bring to rolling boil. Remove from heat and immediately add tapioca flour. Mix quickly with wooden spoon. Cool 5 minutes.

3. Place mixture in food processor and add egg, cheese, and salt. Process until mixture is smooth and forms ball.

4. With 1 ½ or 2-inch spring-action ice cream scoop, drop 12 balls of dough onto ungreased baking sheet about 2 inches apart. For smoother balls, roll each between your oiled palms.

5. Bake 30 to 35 minutes or until balls are lightly browned and crisp. Makes 12. Serve warm or at room temperature.
Calories: 190; Fat 10g; Protein 4g; Carbohydrates 22g; Sodium 190mg; Cholesterol 33mg; Fiber 0g

Cheese Bread Sandwich Buns: Shape dough into 8 balls and flatten slightly with wet spatula before baking as directed. Turn buns over midway through baking.

⋙· Corn Bread ·⋘

For a lighter texture, sift dry ingredients together after measuring. Gluten-free brands of cornmeal include Albers, Lamb's, Kinnikinnick, and Shiloh Farms.

1 ¼ cups cornmeal
1 cup Flour Blend (page 41)
⅓ cup sugar
2 teaspoons baking powder
1 ½ teaspoons xanthan gum

1 teaspoon salt
2 large eggs, lightly beaten
1 cup milk (cow, rice, soy)
⅓ cup canola oil

1. Preheat oven to 350°F. Grease 8 x 4-inch or 8-inch round or square nonstick pan. Or, use 10-inch cast-iron skillet. Set aside.

2. In medium bowl, combine dry ingredients (cornmeal through salt). Make well in center.

3. In another bowl, beat eggs, milk, and oil until well blended. Add egg mixture all at once to dry mixture, stirring just until moist. Batter will be consistency of thick cake batter.

4. Bake 25 to 30 minutes or until top is firm and edges are lightly browned. Serve warm. Serves 12.

Calories 180; Fat 7g; Protein 3g; Carbohydrates 28g; Cholesterol 2mg; Sodium 242mg; Fiber 1g

---

 Carol's Tip: Use a cast iron skillet for a crispier crust on your corn bread.

○ॐ• Focaccia •🙸

Focaccia is a cross between pizza and Italian flatbread. This is undoubtedly one of my most popular recipes!

Bread
1 ½ teaspoons active dry yeast
1 ½ cups Flour Blend (page 41)
1 ½ teaspoon xanthan gum
1 teaspoon unflavored gelatin powder
1 teaspoon dried rosemary
½ teaspoon onion powder
¾ teaspoon salt
¾ cup warm (110°F) water

1 teaspoon sugar
2 large eggs
2 tablespoons olive oil
½ teaspoon cider vinegar

Topping
1 tablespoon olive oil
1 ¼ teaspoon Italian seasoning
¼ teaspoon kosher or coarse sea salt

1. Combine all bread ingredients in mixing bowl. Beat dough with mixer (regular beaters, not dough hooks) for 1 minute. Dough will be soft and sticky.

2. Transfer dough to greased 11 x 7-inch nonstick pan. Cover with aluminum foil tent and let rise in warm place (75 to 80°F) for 30 to 40 minutes or until desired height.

3. Preheat oven to 400°F. Sprinkle dough with topping ingredients. Bake 15 to 20 minutes or until top is golden brown. (A sprinkle of Parmesan cheese is optional.) Serves 10.

Calories 110; Fat 5g; Protein 2g; Carbohydrates 17g; Cholesterol 06mg; Sodium 244mg; Fiber 1g

Muffaletta (Sandwiches): Bake in greased 10-inch springform pan until deep, golden brown. Cool; remove from pan. Slice loaf in half, horizontally. Pull out some of insides with your hands, leaving shell 1-inch thick. Brush bottom with olive oil, mayonnaise, mustard, or sauces. Layer with sandwich fillings: cheese, ham, tomatoes, olives, and more sauce. Replace top. Wrap loosely in foil; heat 20 minutes at 400°F on baking sheet. Slice with electric knife to serve. Makes 6.

‹§• French Bread •ü›

Put this bread into a COLD oven for a crisp crust and nice texture. If this doesn't work in your oven, let the bread rise until level with top of pan; then bake in preheated 425°F oven 25 to 30 minutes. Use a pan specially designed for French bread. Use dry milk powder found in natural food stores, not Carnation.

2 tablespoons active dry yeast
1 ¼ cups warm (110°F) water
1 tablespoon sugar
2 cups Flour Blend (page 41)
1 cup potato starch
1 teaspoon xanthan gum
1 teaspoon guar gum

¼ cup dry milk powder (cow, rice, soy)
1 ¼ to 2 teaspoons salt
1 tablespoon soft butter/canola oil
3 large egg whites
1 teaspoon cider vinegar
Egg white wash (optional:1 egg white, beaten)

1. Dissolve sugar and yeast in warm water. Set aside 5 minutes.

2. Grease French bread pans or line with parchment paper.

3. In bowl of heavy-duty stand mixer, combine all ingredients (flour through vinegar) plus yeast-water mixture. Beat on low speed to blend. Beat on high speed for 1 minute, stirring down sides with spatula. Dough will be soft.

4. Divide dough in half on prepared pan. Smooth each half into 12-inch log with wet spatula. Brush with egg wash for glossier crust. Make 3 diagonal slashes (⅛-inch deep) in each loaf so steam can escape during rising.

5. Place immediately on middle rack in *cold* oven. Set to 425°F and bake approximately 30 to 35 minutes, or until nicely browned.

6. Remove bread from pans; cool completely on wire rack before slicing with electric knife. Makes 2 loaves. Serves 20 (1-inch slices).
Calories 83; Fat 1g; Protein 2g; Carbohydrates 17g; Sodium 159mg; Cholesterol 2mg; Fiber <1g

Dinner Rolls (stand alone style): Use spring-action ice cream scoop to drop 18 mounds of dough on two parchment-lined baking sheets (9 rolls per sheet). Put in cold oven; set temperature to 400°F. Bake on middle rack 20 to 25 minutes or until browned.

ೞ• Hamburger Buns •ಬ

Fire up the grill for hamburgers! These easy buns won't crumble and they freeze well.

1 ½ teaspoons active dry yeast
2 teaspoons sugar
1 cup warm (110°F) water
1 ½ cups Flour Blend (page 41)
1 tablespoon dried minced onion
2 teaspoons xanthan gum
1 teaspoon unflavored gelatin powder

1 teaspoon baking powder
¾ teaspoon salt
¼ teaspoon soy lecithin (optional)
2 tablespoons melted butter/canola oil
2 large eggs
½ teaspoon cider vinegar

1. Combine yeast and sugar with warm water. Set aside 5 minutes.

2. Combine dry ingredients (flour through lecithin) in mixer bowl. Add remaining ingredients. Beat dough with electric mixer on high (using regular beaters, not dough hooks) for 1 minute. Dough will be very soft and sticky.

3. Transfer dough to eight greased English muffin rings (or foil rings—see below) on baking sheet. Spread dough to edges with wet spatula. Cover; let rise in warm place 20 to 30 minutes or until dough is just below top of ring.

4. Preheat oven to 350°F. Bake 15 to 20 minutes or until tops are golden brown and firm. Cool 5 minutes; remove buns from rings. Lightly toast cut side of bun before serving for a crispy texture. Makes 8 buns. Serves 8.
Calories 135; Fat 5g; Protein 3g; Carbohydrates 22g; Sodium 265mg; Cholesterol 61mg; Fiber 1g

Hot Dog Buns: Fill hot-dog shaped foil rings or specially-designed hotdog pans with dough.

Herb Buns: Add 1 teaspoon rosemary leaves (crushed) and ½ teaspoon Italian herb seasoning.

Foil Rings: Tear off 12-inch strip of aluminum foil. Fold over and over lengthwise in 1-inch folds. Fashion into hamburger bun or hotdog bun shape and secure with masking tape.

◌ Popovers ◌

The secret to successful popovers is having the ingredients at room temperature and heating the pans before baking. Popovers are great for sandwiches, too.

4 large eggs
¾ cup milk (cow, rice, soy)
1 tablespoon canola oil
⅔ cup potato starch

¼ cup Flour Blend (page 41)
½ teaspoon salt
¼ teaspoon xanthan gum

1. Adjust oven rack to lower-middle position. Preheat oven to 450°F. Have all ingredients at room temperature. Thoroughly blend all ingredients in blender.

2. Place 6-muffin or popover pan, or 6 custard cups in oven three minutes while pre-heating. Just before pouring batter into pan, remove pan from oven and generously coat with cooking spray.

3. Fill pan or cups three-fourths full. Bake 20 minutes at 450°F, then reduce heat to 350°F and continue baking 15 minutes more or until sides of muffins are rigid. Do not open oven until five minutes before popovers are done baking. Pierce each popover with toothpick; return to oven five more minutes. Serve warm. Makes 6. Serves 6.

Calories 150; Fat 6g; Protein 5g; Carbohydrates 18g; Sodium 250mg; Cholesterol 144mg; Fiber <1g

Yorkshire Pudding: Pour 1 teaspoon of hot meat drippings into each cup or pan. Add popover batter and bake as directed above. Serves 6.

Calories 190; Fat 11g; Protein 5g; Carbohydrates 18g; Sodium 277mg; Cholesterol 148mg.; Fiber <1g

☙ Potato Bread ❧

So many of you asked for an old-fashioned potato bread recipe—I just had to include it in this book. It's a great way to use up leftover mashed potatoes. Use dry milk powder found in natural food stores, not Carnation.

2 teaspoons active dry yeast	¾ teaspoon salt
¾ cup water or potato water*	⅓ cup dry milk powder (cow, rice, soy)
2 tablespoons sugar, divided	¼ teaspoon soy lecithin (optional)
1 cup potato starch	2 large eggs
½ cup Flour Blend (page 41)	½ cup mashed potatoes
½ cup tapioca flour	¼ cup melted butter/canola oil
2 teaspoons xanthan gum	1 teaspoon cider vinegar

*water used to boil potatoes

1. Have all ingredients at room temperature. Combine yeast, 2 teaspoons of the sugar, and warm (110°F) water. Set aside to let yeast foam, about 5 minutes.

2. In large mixer bowl using regular beaters (not dough hooks), combine all ingredients. Beat on medium speed for 1 minute.

3. For smaller loaves, generously grease three small 5 x 3-inch pans,. Divide dough among pans and let rise in warm place (75 to 80ºF) until dough is level with top of pan (no higher), about 25 to 30 minutes.

4. For one large loaf, use generously greased 8 x 4-inch pan. Let rise in warm place (75 to 80ºF) until dough is level with top of pan (no higher), about 45 to 60 minutes.

5. Preheat oven to 375ºF. Bake small loaves for 25 to 30 minutes; large loaf for 45 to 50 minutes, or until nicely browned and internal temperature is 205°F on an instant-read thermometer. Makes a 1 pound loaf. Serves 12.

Calories 140; Fat 5g; Protein 2g; Carbohydrates 25g; Sodium 194mg; Cholesterol 46mg; Fiber <1g

Breakfast & Brunch

For more delicious breads see:

Wheat-Free Recipes & Menus: Delicious, Healthful Eating for People with Food Sensitivities by Carol Fenster, Ph.D.
Cooking Free: 200 Flavorful Recipes for People with Food Allergies & Multiple Food Sensitivities by Carol Fenster, Ph.D.
Gluten-Free Quick & Easy--From Prep to Plate without the Fuss by Carol Fenster, Ph.D.
1,000 Gluten-Free Recipes by Carol Fenster, Ph.D.

ભ• Bagels •ও

Bagels are actually quite easy. With a little practice, you'll be a pro! Use dry milk powder found in natural food stores, not Carnation.

⅔ cup warm (110°F) water
4 teaspoons active dry yeast
2 tablespoons sugar, divided
1 cup Flour Blend (page 41)
1 cup potato starch
½ cup dry milk powder (cow, rice, soy)

2 teaspoons salt
2 teaspoons xanthan gum
1 teaspoon guar gum
1 tablespoon canola oil
1 large egg
1 teaspoon cider vinegar

1. Dissolve yeast and 1 tablespoon sugar in warm water. Grease large baking sheet or line with parchment paper.

2. Combine all ingredients (and remaining sugar) in mixing bowl of heavy-duty stand mixer. Beat with regular beaters on medium speed for 1 minute. Dough will be stiff.

3. Divide dough into 8 equal portions. Generously dust each portion with rice flour; then shape into ball. Flatten to 3-inch circle, dust again, and punch hole in center. Pull gently to make bagel shape with 1-inch diameter. Place on sheet.

4. Place bagels in *cold* oven; turn to 325°F. Bake 10 minutes.

5. Meanwhile, bring 3 inches water, 1 tablespoon sugar, and 1 tablespoon oil to boil in large pan on stovetop. Boil bagels 30 seconds. (Leave oven on.)

6. Return baking sheet to oven; increase temperature to 350°F. Bake 25 to 30 minutes, or until browned. Cool on rack. Makes 8.

Calories 165; Fat 3g; Protein 4g; Carbohydrates 33g; Sodium 614mg; Cholesterol 27mg; Fiber <1g

Onion Bagels: Add 1 tablespoon dried minced onions to dough.

ಇ⁂ Cinnamon-Currant Bagels ⁂ಇ

This is my husband's favorite flavor of bagels. Use dry milk powder found in natural food stores, not Carnation.

⅔ cup warm (110°F) water
4 teaspoons active dry yeast
3 tablespoons sugar, divided
1 cup Flour Blend (page 41)
1 cup potato starch
½ cup dry milk powder (cow, rice, soy)
2 teaspoons ground cinnamon

2 teaspoons salt
2 teaspoons xanthan gum
1 teaspoon guar gum
1 tablespoon canola oil
1 large egg
1 teaspoon cider vinegar
½ cup currants (or raisins)

1. Dissolve yeast and 1 tablespoon sugar in warm water. Grease large baking sheet or line with parchment paper.

2. Combine all ingredients (and 1 tablespoon of remaining sugar) in mixing bowl of heavy-duty stand mixer. Beat with regular beaters on medium speed for 1 minute. Dough will be stiff.

3. Divide dough into 8 equal portions. Generously dust each portion with rice flour; then shape into ball. Flatten to 3-inch circle, dust again, and punch hole in center. Pull gently to make bagel shape with 1-inch diameter. Place on sheet.

4. Place bagels in *cold* oven; turn to 325°F. Bake 10 minutes.

5. Meanwhile, bring 3 inches water, 1 tablespoon sugar, and 1 tablespoon oil to boil in large pan on stovetop. Boil bagels 30 seconds. (Leave oven on.)

6. Return baking sheet to oven; increase temperature to 350°F. Bake 25 to 30 minutes, or until browned. Cool on rack. Makes 8.

Calories 195; Fat 3g; Protein 4g; Carbohydrates 41g; Sodium 614mg; Cholesterol 27mg; Fiber <1g

ೞ• Onion Bagels •ಜಿ

This version is especially good as a base for savory sandwiches or with lox and cream cheese. Use dry milk powder found in natural food stores, not Carnation.

⅔ cup warm (110°F) water
4 teaspoons active dry yeast
2 tablespoons sugar, divided
1 cup Flour Blend (page 41)
1 cup potato starch
½ cup dry milk powder (cow, rice, soy)
1 tablespoon dried minced onion

2 teaspoons salt
2 teaspoons xanthan gum
1 teaspoon guar gum
1 tablespoon canola oil
1 large egg
1 teaspoon cider vinegar

1. Dissolve yeast and 1 tablespoon sugar in warm water. Grease large baking sheet or line with parchment paper.

2. Combine all ingredients (and remaining sugar) in mixing bowl of heavy-duty stand mixer. Beat with regular beaters on medium speed for 1 minute. Dough will be stiff.

3. Divide dough into 8 equal portions. Generously dust each portion with rice flour; then shape into ball. Flatten to 3-inch circle, dust again, and punch hole in center. Pull gently to make bagel shape with 1-inch diameter. Place on sheet.

4. Place bagels in *cold* oven; turn to 325°F. Bake 10 minutes.

5. Meanwhile, bring 3 inches water, 1 tablespoon sugar, and 1 tablespoon oil to boil in large pan on stovetop. Boil bagels 30 seconds. (Leave oven on.)

6. Return baking sheet to oven; increase temperature to 350°F. Bake 25 to 30 minutes, or until browned. Cool on rack. Makes 8.

Calories 165; Fat 3g; Protein 4g; Carbohydrates 33g; Sodium 614mg; Cholesterol 27mg; Fiber <1g

ಬ• Basic Muffins •ಜ

Use this recipe when you want a plain, unflavored muffin or one to add your own flavorings to. For recipes for flavored muffins, see pages 84 to 90.

Dry Ingredients
2 ⅓ cups Flour Blend (page 41)
⅔ cup sugar
1 tablespoon baking powder
1 ½ teaspoons xanthan gum
1 teaspoon unflavored gelatin powder
1 teaspoon salt

Wet Ingredients
1 cup milk (cow, rice, soy)
¼ cup canola oil
2 large eggs
1 teaspoon vanilla extract

1. Preheat oven to 375ºF. Generously grease standard 12-cup non-stick standard muffin pan.

2. Whisk or sift together dry ingredients in large bowl. In separate bowl, whisk wet ingredients thoroughly until smooth.

3. Make well in dry ingredients and add wet ingredients. Combine until just moistened.

4. Divide batter evenly in pan. Bake approximately 20 to 25 minutes or until muffin tops are lightly browned. Makes 12.
Calories 195; Fat 6g; Protein 3g; Carbohydrates 33g; Sodium 273mg; Cholesterol 37mg; Fiber <1g

 Carol's Tip: Gray, nonstick muffin pans produce the best muffin crust. Black muffin pans tend to burn the muffins; shiny aluminum pans don't brown them enough.

ເຮ• Banana Chocolate Chip Muffins •ຮວ

If you love bananas and chocolate—as I do—you'll love this version of easy muffins.

Dry Ingredients
2 ⅓ cups Flour Blend (page 41)
⅔ cup sugar
1 tablespoon baking powder
1 ½ teaspoons ground cinnamon
1 ½ teaspoon xanthan gum
1 teaspoon salt

Wet Ingredients
½ cup milk (cow, rice, soy)
¼ cup canola oil
2 large eggs
2 mashed medium ripe bananas
1 teaspoon vanilla extract

1 cup gluten-free chocolate chips

1. Preheat oven to 375°F. Generously grease standard 12-cup non-stick standard muffin pan.

2. Whisk or sift together dry ingredients in large bowl. In separate bowl, whisk wet ingredients thoroughly until smooth.

3. Make well in dry ingredients and add wet ingredients. Combine until just moistened. Gently stir in chocolate chips.

4. Divide batter evenly in pan. Bake approximately 20 to 25 minutes or until muffin tops are lightly browned. Makes 12.

Calories 280; Fat 11g; Protein 4g; Carbohydrates 45g; Sodium 280mg; Cholesterol 39mg; Fiber 2g

ತಞ• Blueberry Lemon Muffins •ಞ

Lemon peel boosts the flavor of blueberries and adds a wonderful citrus scent to these muffins.

Dry Ingredients	Wet Ingredients
Dry Ingredients	**Wet Ingredients**
2 ⅓ cups Flour Blend (page 41)	1 cup milk (cow, rice, soy)
⅔ cup sugar	¼ cup canola oil
1 tablespoon baking powder	2 large eggs
1 ½ teaspoons xanthan gum	1 tablespoon grated lemon peel
1 teaspoon unflavored gelatin powder	1 teaspoon vanilla extract
1 teaspoon salt	

1 cup fresh blueberries

1. Preheat oven to 375°F. Generously grease standard 12-cup non-stick standard muffin pan.

2. Whisk or sift together dry ingredients in large bowl. In separate bowl, whisk wet ingredients thoroughly until smooth.

3. Make well in dry ingredients and add wet ingredients. Combine until just moistened. Gently fold in blueberries.

4. Divide batter evenly in pan. Bake approximately 20 to 25 minutes or until muffin tops are lightly browned. Makes 12.

Calories 205; Fat 6g; Protein 3g; Carbohydrates 35g; Sodium 274mg; Cholesterol 37mg; Fiber 1g

✂• Bran Spice Muffins •✂

These muffins make a hearty breakfast choice and also travel very well.

Dry Ingredients
2 cups Flour Blend (page 41)
⅔ cup light brown sugar, packed
⅓ cup rice bran
1 tablespoon baking powder
1 ½ teaspoons ground cinnamon
1 ½ teaspoons xanthan gum
1 teaspoon unflavored gelatin powder
1 teaspoon salt
½ teaspoon ground nutmeg
¼ teaspoon ground cloves
¼ teaspoon ground allspice

Wet Ingredients
1 cup milk (cow, rice, soy)
¼ cup canola oil
2 large eggs
1 tablespoon molasses
1 teaspoon vanilla extract

½ cup dark raisins

1. Preheat oven to 375°F. Generously grease standard 12-cup non-stick standard muffin pan.

2. Whisk or sift together dry ingredients in large bowl. In separate bowl, whisk wet ingredients thoroughly until smooth.

3. Make well in dry ingredients and add wet ingredients. Combine until just moistened. Gently stir in raisins.

4. Divide batter evenly in pan. Bake approximately 20 to 25 minutes or until muffin tops are lightly browned. Makes 12.

Calories 230; Fat 7g; Protein 4g; Carbohydrates 41g; Sodium 275mg; Cholesterol 37mg; Fiber 2g

ೞ• Cranberry Orange Muffins •ಜ

The cranberry and orange flavors are a hit for brunch at holiday time.

Dry Ingredients
2 ⅓ cups Flour Blend (page 41)
⅔ cup sugar
1 tablespoon baking powder
1 ½ teaspoons xanthan gum
1 teaspoon unflavored gelatin powder
1 teaspoon salt

Wet Ingredients
1 cup milk (cow, rice, soy)
¼ cup canola oil
2 large eggs
1 tablespoon grated orange peel
1 teaspoon vanilla extract

1 cup chopped fresh cranberries

1. Preheat oven to 375°F. Generously grease standard 12-cup non-stick standard muffin pan.

2. Whisk or sift together dry ingredients in large bowl. In separate bowl, whisk wet ingredients thoroughly until smooth.

3. Make well in dry ingredients and add wet ingredients. Combine until just moistened. Gently stir in cranberries. (You may use dried, sweetened cranberries instead but this will add calories and carbohydrates.)

4. Divide batter evenly in pan. Bake approximately 20 to 25 minutes or until muffin tops are lightly browned. Makes 12.
Calories 200; Fat 6g; Protein 3g; Carbohydrates 33g; Sodium 273mg; Cholesterol 37mg; Fiber 1g

↢• Lemon Dried Cranberry Muffins •↣

Lots of citrusy lemon permeates this muffin and the cranberries add a nice texture.

Dry Ingredients
2 ⅓ cups Flour Blend (page 41)
⅔ cup sugar
1 tablespoon baking powder
1 ½ teaspoons xanthan gum
1 teaspoon unflavored gelatin powder
1 teaspoon salt

Wet Ingredients
1 cup milk (cow, rice, soy)
¼ cup canola oil
2 large eggs
2 tablespoons grated lemon peel
1 teaspoon vanilla extract

1 cup dried sweetened cranberries

1. Preheat oven to 375°F. Generously grease standard 12-cup non-stick standard muffin pan.

2. Whisk or sift together dry ingredients in large bowl. In separate bowl, whisk wet ingredients thoroughly until smooth.

3. Make well in dry ingredients and add wet ingredients. Combine until just moistened. Gently stir in dried, sweetened cranberries.

4. Divide batter evenly in pan. Bake approximately 20 to 25 minutes or until muffin tops are lightly browned. Makes 12.

Calories 230; Fat 6g; Protein 3g; Carbohydrates 39g; Sodium 273mg; Cholesterol 37mg; Fiber 2g

෫• Lemon Poppy Seed Muffins •෫

It seems like those of us who grew up in the Midwest really enjoy our poppy seeds. They make these muffins taste like the old-fashioned muffins I ate when I was growing up.

Dry Ingredients
2 ⅓ cups Flour Blend (page 41)
⅔ cup sugar
1 tablespoon poppy seeds
1 tablespoon baking powder
1 ½ teaspoons xanthan gum
1 teaspoon unflavored gelatin powder
1 teaspoon salt

Wet Ingredients
1 cup milk (cow, rice, or soy)
¼ cup canola oil
2 large eggs
2 tablespoons grated lemon peel
1 teaspoon vanilla extract

1. Preheat oven to 375°F. Generously grease standard 12-cup non-stick standard muffin pan.

2. Whisk or sift together dry ingredients in large bowl. In separate bowl, whisk wet ingredients thoroughly until smooth.

3. Make well in dry ingredients and add wet ingredients. Combine until just moistened.

4. Divide batter evenly in pan. Bake approximately 20 to 25 minutes or until muffin tops are lightly browned. Makes 12.

Calories:195; Fat 6g; Protein 3g; Carbohydrates 33g; Sodium 273mg; Cholesterol 37mg; Fiber <1g

ଓଃ• Raspberry Muffins •ଞ

Succulent raspberries add a special touch to these muffins.

Dry Ingredients
2 ⅓ cups Flour Blend (page 41)
⅔ cup sugar
1 tablespoon baking powder
1 ½ teaspoons xanthan gum
1 teaspoon ground cinnamon
1 teaspoon unflavored gelatin powder
1 teaspoon salt

Wet Ingredients
1 cup milk (cow, rice, soy)
¼ cup canola oil
2 large eggs
1 teaspoon vanilla extract

1 ¼ cups fresh raspberries

1. Preheat oven to 375°F. Generously grease standard 12-cup non-stick standard muffin pan.

2. Whisk or sift together dry ingredients in large bowl. In separate bowl, whisk wet ingredients thoroughly until smooth.

3. Make well in dry ingredients and add wet ingredients. Combine until just moistened. Gently stir in fresh raspberries.

4. Divide batter evenly in pan. Bake approximately 20 to 25 minutes or until muffin tops are lightly browned. Makes 12.

Calories 205; Fat 6g; Protein 3g; Carbohydrates 34g; Sodium 273mg; Cholesterol 37mg; Fiber 2g

☙• Basic Quick Bread •❧

The simple bread is great and can be made in many ways, such as adding nuts, chopped fruit, or dried fruits such as raisins.

Wet Ingredients
¼ cup canola oil
2 large eggs
1 teaspoon vanilla extract
1 cup milk (cow, rice, soy)
1 teaspoon grated lemon peel

Dry Ingredients
2 ⅓ cups Flour Blend (page 41)
1 ½ teaspoons xanthan gum
1 teaspoon unflavored gelatin powder
2 ½ teaspoons baking powder
1 teaspoon salt
⅔ cup sugar

1. Preheat oven to 375ºF. Grease three 5 x 3-inch nonstick pans.

2. Thoroughly blend all wet ingredients with electric mixer in mixing bowl. Sift together dry ingredients and thoroughly mix with liquid ingredients.

3. Gently stir in fruit or nuts (if using). Spoon batter into pans.

4. Bake 35 to 40 minutes or until top is nicely browned. Remove from oven. Cool pan on wire rack for 10 minutes. Remove bread from pan and finish cooling on wire rack. Cut into 24 slices. Serves 12 (2 slices each).
Calories 200; Fat 6g; Protein 3g; Carbohydrates 33g; Sodium 237mg; Cholesterol 37mg; Fiber <1g

 Carol's Tip: A well-known cooking magazine found that inexpensive nonstick pans sold in supermarkets produce superior baked goods over the more expensive, gourmet store brands.

ॐ• Banana Bread •৪০

Whenever I have bananas that are extra-ripe, I make banana bread. It freezes and travels very well.

Wet Ingredients	**Dry Ingredients**
¼ cup canola oil	2 ⅓ cups Flour Blend (page 41)
2 large eggs	⅔ cup light brown sugar, packed
1 teaspoon vanilla extract	1 ½ teaspoons xanthan gum
1 cup milk (cow, rice, soy)	2 ½ teaspoons baking powder
2 mashed ripe medium bananas	1 ½ teaspoons ground cinnamon
	1 teaspoon salt

½ cups chopped walnuts
½ cups dark raisins

1. Preheat oven to 375ºF. Grease three 5 x 3-inch nonstick pans.

2. Thoroughly blend all wet ingredients with electric mixer in mixing bowl. Sift together dry ingredients and thoroughly mix with liquid ingredients.

3. Gently stir in nuts and raisins. Spoon batter into pans.

4. Bake 35 to 40 minutes or until top is nicely browned. Remove from oven. Cool pan on wire rack for 10 minutes. Remove bread from pan and finish cooling on wire rack. Cut into 24 slices. Serves 12 (2 slices each).

Calories 272; Fat 10g; Protein 4g; Carbohydrates 44g; Sodium 241mg; Cholesterol 38mg; Fiber 2g

Blueberry Lemon Bread

The simple bread is great and can be made in many ways.

Wet Ingredients

¼ cup canola oil
2 large eggs
1 teaspoon vanilla extract
1 cup milk (cow, rice, soy)
2 teaspoons grated lemon peel

Dry Ingredients

2 ⅓ cups Flour Blend (page 41)
1 ½ teaspoons xanthan gum
1 teaspoon unflavored gelatin powder
2 ½ teaspoons baking powder
1 teaspoon salt
⅔ cup sugar

1 ¼ cups fresh blueberries

1. Preheat oven to 375°F. Grease three 5 x 3-inch nonstick pans.

2. Thoroughly blend all wet ingredients with electric mixer in mixing bowl. Sift together dry ingredients and thoroughly mix with liquid ingredients.

3. Gently stir in blueberries. Spoon batter into pans.

4. Bake 35 to 40 minutes or until top is nicely browned. You may have to bake this bread 5 to 10 minutes longer if you use frozen blueberries. Remove from oven. Cool pan on wire rack for 10 minutes. Remove bread from pan and finish cooling on wire rack. Cut into 24 slices. Serves 12 (2 slices each).

Calories 205; Fat 6g; Protein 3g; Carbohydrates 35g; Sodium 238mg; Cholesterol 37mg; Fiber 1g

∽• Cranberry Orange Bread •∾

The flavors of cranberry and orange seem to be made for each other.

Wet Ingredients	Dry Ingredients
¼ cup canola oil	2 ⅓ cups Flour Blend (page 41)
2 large eggs	1 ½ teaspoons xanthan gum
1 teaspoon vanilla extract	1 teaspoon unflavored gelatin powder
1 cup milk (cow, rice, soy)	2 ½ teaspoons baking powder
1 teaspoon grated lemon peel	1 teaspoon salt
1 tablespoon grated orange peel	⅔ cup sugar

1 ½ cups chopped fresh cranberries

1. Preheat oven to 375°F. Grease three 5 x 3-inch nonstick pans.

2. Thoroughly blend all wet ingredients with electric mixer in mixing bowl. Sift together dry ingredients and thoroughly mix with liquid ingredients.

3. Gently stir in fruit or nuts (if using). Spoon batter into pans.

4. Bake 35 to 40 minutes or until top is nicely browned. Remove from oven. Cool pan on wire rack for 10 minutes. Remove bread from pan and finish cooling on wire rack. Cut into 24 slices. Serves 12 (2 slices each).

Calories 200; Fat 6g; Protein 3g; Carbohydrates 34g; Sodium 237mg; Cholesterol 37mg; Fiber 1g

ℭℨ• Pumpkin Raisin Bread •℞

This hearty quick bread makes your kitchen smell absolutely heavenly.

Wet Ingredients
¼ cup canola oil
2 large eggs
1 teaspoon vanilla extract
1 cup milk (cow, rice, soy)
½ cup canned pumpkin

Dry Ingredients
2 ⅓ cups Flour Blend (page 41)
⅔ cup sugar
2 ½ teaspoons baking powder
1 ½ teaspoons pumpkin pie spice
1 ½ teaspoons xanthan gum
1 teaspoon unflavored gelatin powder
1 teaspoon salt
¼ teaspoon ground allspice
¼ teaspoon ground ginger
1 ½ cups golden raisins

1. Preheat oven to 375°F. Grease three 5 x 3-inch nonstick pans.

2. Thoroughly blend all wet ingredients with electric mixer in mixing bowl. Sift together dry ingredients and thoroughly blend into liquid ingredients with electric mixer.

3. Gently stir in fruit or nuts (if using). Spoon batter into pans.

4. Bake 35 to 40 minutes or until top is nicely browned. Remove from oven. Cool pan on wire rack for 10 minutes. Remove bread from pan and finish cooling on wire rack. Cut into 24 slices. Serves 12 (2 slices each).
Calories 265; Fat 6g; Protein 4g; Carbohydrates 50g; Sodium 240mg; Cholesterol 37mg; Fiber 2g

❧ Sweet Potato Cranberry Bread ❧

This makes excellent holiday bread and is a great way to use leftover sweet potatoes.

Wet Ingredients
¼ cup canola oil
2 large eggs
1 teaspoon vanilla extract
1 cup milk (cow, rice, soy)
½ cup mashed sweet potato

Dry Ingredients
2 ⅓ cups Flour Blend (page 41)
1 ½ teaspoons xanthan gum
1 teaspoon unflavored gelatin powder
2 ½ teaspoons baking powder
1 teaspoon salt
⅔ cup sugar
1 ½ teaspoons pumpkin pie spice

1 cup dried sweetened cranberries

1. Preheat oven to 375°F. Grease three 5 x 3-inch nonstick pans.

2. Thoroughly blend all wet ingredients with electric mixer in mixing bowl. Sift together dry ingredients and thoroughly mix with liquid ingredients.

3. Gently stir in cranberries. Spoon batter into pans.

4. Bake 35 to 40 minutes or until top is nicely browned. Remove from oven. Cool pan on wire rack for 10 minutes. Remove bread from pan and finish cooling on wire rack. Cut into 24 slices. Serves 12 (2 slices each).
Calories 245; Fat 6g; Protein 3g; Carbohydrates 45g; Sodium 238mg; Cholesterol 37mg; Fiber 2g

ଔ• Biscuits •ଓ

Biscuits are the ultimate comfort food. Serve them warm with butter and honey, or your favorite jam or jelly. Top them with creamy gravy for old-fashioned Biscuits & Gravy. I prefer using parchment paper rather than greasing the baking sheet.

1 cup Flour Blend (page 41)
½ cup cornstarch or potato starch
1 tablespoon sugar
2 teaspoons baking powder
¼ teaspoon baking soda
1 teaspoon xanthan gum

1 teaspoon guar gum
½ teaspoon salt
¼ cup shortening*
½ cup milk (cow, rice, soy)
1 large egg white

Non-hydrogenated shortenings by Spectrum® and Smart Balance® are available at health food stores.

1. Preheat oven to 350°F. Grease baking sheet or line with parchment paper. Dust surface lightly with cornstarch.

2. In food processor, pulse dry ingredients (cornstarch through salt) to mix thoroughly. Add shortening, milk, and egg white. Blend until dough forms ball, scraping down sides with spatula, if necessary. Dough will be somewhat soft.

3. Place dough on prepared baking sheet. Lightly dust dough with cornstarch. Gently pat to ¾-inch thick circle. Cut into ten 2-inch circles with floured biscuit cutter. Push the biscuit cutter straight down on dough rather than twisting it as you cut. Shape remaining dough to ¾-inch thick and cut again. If dough is sticky, lightly dust with more cornstarch. Arrange evenly on baking sheet.

4. Bake 12 to 15 minutes or until nicely browned. Serve immediately. Serves 10.
Calories: 130; Fat 6g; Protein 1g; Carbohydrates 19g; Sodium 206mg; Cholesterol <1mg; Fiber <1g

Carol's Tip: Parchment paper works great for cut-outs such as biscuits. It prevents sticking, plus you can shape the biscuits on parchment paper on the counter top; then transfer paper (with biscuits on it) to the baking sheet. Or, as I do—cut out the biscuits right on the parchment-lined baking sheet.

෬• Cinnamon Coffee Cake •ෞ

I've served this easy breakfast treat to many a delighted gluten-free guest.

¾ cup sugar
2 large eggs
¼ cup canola oil
1 tablespoon lemon peel
1 teaspoon vanilla extract
1 ½ cups Flour Blend (page 41)

1 ½ teaspoons xanthan gum
½ teaspoon baking powder
½ teaspoon baking soda
½ teaspoon salt
⅔ cup buttermilk or 2 teaspoons
  vinegar plus milk (cow, rice, soy)
  to equal ⅔ cup.

Cinnamon Crumb Topping

¼ cup packed light brown sugar
2 tablespoons butter or
  margarine

½ teaspoon ground cinnamon
⅓ cup Flour Blend (page 41)

1. Preheat oven to 350ºF. Grease 11 x 7-inch nonstick pan.

2. Using electric mixer and large mixer bowl, cream together the sugar, eggs, and oil about 1 minute. Add grated peel and vanilla.

3. In a medium bowl, sift together flours, xanthan gum, baking powder, baking soda, and salt.

4. On low speed, beat dry ingredients into egg mixture, alternating with buttermilk mixture, beginning and ending with dry ingredients. Spoon batter into pan; put topping on batter.

5. Bake 35 minutes or until top is golden brown and cake tester comes out clean. Serves 10.

Calories 250; Fat 8g; Protein 3g; Carbohydrates 45g; Sodium 201mg; Cholesterol 36mg; Fiber <1g

∞• Cranberry-Orange Coffee Cake •∞

You'll love this easy, flavorful treat that's great for guests or for your family, anytime.

¾ cup sugar
2 large eggs
¼ cup canola oil
1 tablespoon orange peel
1 teaspoon vanilla extract
1 ½ cups Flour Blend (page 41)
1 ½ teaspoons xanthan gum

½ teaspoon baking powder
½ teaspoon baking soda
½ teaspoon salt
⅔ cup buttermilk or 2 teaspoons
   vinegar plus milk (cow, rice, soy)
   to equal ⅔ cup.
1 cup fresh cranberries, chopped

Cinnamon Crumb Topping

¼ cup packed light brown sugar
2 tablespoons butter/canola oil

½ teaspoon ground cinnamon
⅓ cup Flour Blend (page 41)

1. Preheat oven to 350ºF. Grease 11 x 7-inch nonstick pan.

2. Using electric mixer and large mixer bowl, cream together the sugar, eggs, and oil about 1 minute. Add grated peel and vanilla.

3. In a medium bowl, sift together flours, xanthan gum, baking powder, baking soda, and salt.

4. On low speed, beat dry ingredients into egg mixture, alternating with buttermilk mixture, beginning and ending with dry ingredients. Gently stir in cranberries. Spoon batter into pan and sprinkle topping on batter.

5. Bake 35 minutes or until top is golden brown and cake tester comes out clean. Serves 10.

Calories 260; Fat 9g; Protein 3g; Carbohydrates 42g; Sodium 224mg; Cholesterol 49mg; Fiber 1g

ᘓ• Lemon Poppy Seed Cake •ᘔ

You can dress up this tasty cake with a drizzle of white frosting.

¾ cup sugar
2 large eggs
¼ cup canola oil
2 tablespoons lemon peel
2 teaspoons vanilla extract
1 ½ cups Flour Blend (page 41)
1 ½ teaspoons xanthan gum

1 tablespoon poppy seed
½ teaspoon baking powder
½ teaspoon baking soda
½ teaspoon salt
⅔ cup buttermilk or 2 teaspoons
    vinegar plus milk (cow, rice, soy)
    to equal ⅔ cup.

Cinnamon Crumb Topping

¼ cup packed light brown sugar
2 tablespoons butter or margarine

½ teaspoon ground cinnamon
⅓ cup Flour Blend (page 41)

1. Preheat oven to 350°F. Grease 11 x 7-inch nonstick pan.

2. Using electric mixer and large mixer bowl, cream together the sugar, eggs, and oil about 1 minute. Add grated peel and vanilla.

3. In a medium bowl, sift together flours, xanthan gum, baking powder, baking soda, and salt.

4. On low speed, beat dry ingredients into egg mixture, alternating with buttermilk mixture, beginning and ending with dry ingredients. Spoon batter into pan; sprinkle topping on batter.

5. Bake 35 minutes or until top is golden brown and cake tester comes out clean. Serves 10.

Calories 255; Fat 9g; Protein 3g; Carbohydrates 41g; Sodium 224mg; Cholesterol 50mg; Fiber <1g

☙• Breakfast Pizza •❧

Don't let this long list of ingredients intimidate you. It's just a pizza crust with eggs and bacon as the topping. Make the pizza the night before and cut it into 6 serving slices. Microwave a slice in the morning and off you go to work or school! Gluten-free fast food!

Topping	Crust
3 eggs, scrambled with ¼ teaspoon salt	1 tablespoon dry yeast
3 tablespoons finely chopped green onions or 1 tablespoon dried minced onions	⅔ cup warm (110°F) milk (cow, rice, soy)
	½ teaspoon sugar
	⅔ cup garbanzo/fava bean flour)
3 cooked bacon strips (crumbled) or ⅓ cup cooked sausage (crumbled) or finely chopped Canadian bacon	½ cup tapioca flour
	2 teaspoons xanthan gum
	½ teaspoon salt
1 ½ cups shredded cheese—divided (e.g., cow, rice, or soy in cheddar or Monterey jack flavors)	1 teaspoon gelatin powder
	1 teaspoon ground oregano
	1 teaspoon olive oil
2 plum tomatoes, finely chopped	1 teaspoon cider vinegar

Pizza Crust

1. Preheat oven to 425°F. Dissolve yeast and sugar in warm milk for five minutes. In food processor, blend all crust ingredients, including yeast mixture, until ball forms. Dough will be soft.

2. Put mixture into greased 12-inch nonstick pizza pan. Liberally sprinkle rice flour on dough; then press dough on pan with your hands, continuing to dust dough with flour to prevent sticking. Make edges thicker to contain toppings.

3. Bake crust 10 minutes. Remove from oven. Add topping (see below) to crust. Bake another 20 to 25 minutes or until top is nicely browned. Serves 6.

Topping

Sprinkle crust with ½ cup cheese. Arrange tomatoes, eggs (finely chopped), onions, and bacon (or sausage or ham) on top. Add remaining cheese. Bake 10 to 15 minutes or until cheese is melted. Serve warm. Serves 6 (1 slice each).

Calories 250; Fat 15g; Protein 15g; Carbohydrates 16g; Sodium 447mg; Cholesterol 136mg; Fiber 2g

Topping Variations

Try a few black olives or a little feta cheese. Or, dried tomatoes and frozen artichokes. Add a few chopped green chiles for a Southwestern touch.

ભ• Sweet Breakfast Pizza •ଊ

Pizza doesn't have to be a savory dish. Try this sweet version and see for yourself. Make the pizza the night before and cut it into 6 serving slices. Microwave a slice in the morning and off you go! Gluten-free fast food!

Sweet Topping
2 tablespoons sugar
1 tablespoon cornstarch
¼ teaspoon cinnamon
¼ teaspoon salt
½ cup orange juice
2 cups dried fruit (e.g., cherries,
   blueberries, or apricots)
   ½ cup sliced almonds
Dusting of powdered sugar

Pizza Crust
1 tablespoon dry yeast
⅔ cup warm (110°F) milk (cow, rice, soy)
2 ½ teaspoons sugar, divided
⅔ cup garbanzo/fava bean flour)
½ cup tapioca flour
2 teaspoons xanthan gum
½ teaspoon salt
1 teaspoon unflavored gelatin powder
1 teaspoon ground cinnamon
1 teaspoon olive oil
1 teaspoon cider vinegar

Pizza Crust
1. Preheat oven to 425°F. Dissolve yeast and sugar in warm milk for 5 minutes. In food processor, blend all crust ingredients, including yeast mixture, until ball forms. Dough will be soft.

2. Put mixture into greased 12-inch nonstick pizza pan. Liberally sprinkle rice flour on dough; then press dough on pan with your hands, continuing to dust dough with flour to prevent sticking. Make edges thicker to hold toppings.

3. Bake crust 10 minutes. Remove from oven. Add topping (see below) to crust. Bake another 20 to 25 minutes or until top is nicely browned. Serves 6.

Topping
1. Whisk together sugar, cornstarch, cinnamon, and salt in small saucepan over medium heat. Slowly whisk in orange juice until mixture thickens. Remove from heat. Stir in dried fruit. Top pizza crust with fruit mixture.

2. Bake 20 minutes or until crust is nicely browned. Dust with powdered sugar just before serving. Serves 6.

Calories 310; Fat 6g; Protein 7g; Carbohydrates 58g; Sodium 310mg; Cholesterol 2mg; Fiber 5g

ೞ• Whole Grains for Breakfast •ಌ

Cooked grains are an essential and very nutritious component of a healthy, gluten-free diet. In fact, hot cereal is an absolute necessity at breakfast for many of us. Just because you don't eat wheat doesn't mean you can't have cooked cereal.

When it comes to hot cereal, many of us think of rice as our only safe option so we stick with brown rice, white rice, or wild rice. Or, we settle for corn grits (polenta to some of you) because we know that corn is gluten-free.

But there are many other whole grain choices such as nutrient-packed amaranth, buckwheat, millet, and quinoa—topped with sugar, cinnamon, honey, maple syrup, brown sugar, fresh fruit, jam, jelly, or nuts.

The following table gives you basic guidelines on how to cook them. Use salt as you wish. Serves 4.

Grain (1 cup)	Water	Cooking Time
Amaranth	2 cups	15 to 20 minutes
Brown rice	2 ½ cups	30 to 45 minutes
Buckwheat	1 cup	15 to 20 minutes
Corn Grits	3 cups	5 minutes
Millet	3 ½ to 4 cups	35 to 45 minutes
Quinoa	2 cups	15 to 20 minutes
Sorghum*	2 cups	40 to 45 minutes
Wild Rice	4 cups	40 minutes
White Rice	2 cups	15 to 20 minutes

*Soak whole sorghum grains in water overnight. Drain thoroughly. Cook as directed above. Whole grain sorghum is available at www.TwinValleyMills.com.

ɔʒ• Crepes •ʀɔ

Use sweet or savory fillings for these easy crepes.

⅔ cup Flour Blend (page 41)
½ teaspoon xanthan gum
½ teaspoon unflavored gelatin powder
⅛ teaspoon salt

¾ cup milk (cow, rice, soy)
2 large eggs
2 teaspoons canola oil
1 teaspoon vanilla extract

1. Combine all ingredients in blender and process until smooth. If possible, refrigerate (in blender) for about 30 minutes. If not, proceed to heat 8-inch skillet or seasoned crepe pan. Heat crepe pan over medium-high heat until a drop of water dances on the surface.

2. Pour scant 2 tablespoons batter into pan and immediately tilt pan to coat bottom evenly. Cook until underside of crepe is brown; flip crepe and cook other side for about 20 to 30 seconds. (First crepe may need to be discarded.) Repeat with remaining batter.

3. Fill with your favorite crepe filling. Makes about 12 crepes. Serves 6. (2 crepes each)

Per crepe:
Calories 105; Fat 4g; Protein 2g; Carbohydrates 13g; Sodium 82mg; Cholesterol 72mg; Fiber <1g

ભ· English Muffins ·ଔ

English Muffins are not that hard to make. Make a batch and freeze the extras. They defrost quickly and are good eaten on the run! Use dry milk powder found in natural food stores, not Carnation.

2 tablespoons active dry yeast
1 tablespoon sugar
1 ¼ cups warm (110°F) water
2 ⅓ cups Flour Blend (page 41)
2 cups tapioca flour
⅔ cup dry milk powder
  (cow, rice, soy)

3 teaspoons xanthan gum
1 tablespoon unflavored gelatin powder
1 teaspoon salt
¼ teaspoon potato (not starch) flour
¼ cup canola oil
4 large egg whites (room temperature)
1 tablespoon yellow cornmeal

1. Dissolve yeast and sugar in water. Let foam 5 minutes.

2. In large mixer bowl, combine flour blend, tapioca flour, dry milk powder, xanthan gum, gelatin powder, salt, and potato flour. Blend on low; then add oil and egg whites. Mix well. Add yeast mixture and beat on high for 1 minute. Arrange muffin rings on baking sheet that is sprayed with cooking spray and dusted with cornmeal.

3. To make aluminum foil rings, see page 76. Spray rings with cooking spray.

4. Divide dough into 12 equal pieces and press into each ring. Cover and let rise in warm place for about 50 minutes.

5. Preheat oven to 350ºF. Bake muffins 15 minutes or until lightly browned. With spatula, turn muffins (tins and all) over and bake another 10 minutes or until lightly browned.

6. Remove English muffins from baking sheets to cool. When rings are cool enough to handle, remove muffins from rings. Makes 12 English muffins. Serves 12.

Calories 235; Fat 5g; Protein 5g; Carbohydrates 43g; Sodium 236mg; Cholesterol <1mg; Fiber 1g

⋅ French Toast ⋅

This is one of my favorite choices for breakfast. Flavor the egg/milk mixture with a little cinnamon, nutmeg, or perhaps orange juice for a delightful taste. To lower the fat and cholesterol, use 6 egg whites instead of 4 whole eggs.

1 French Bread loaf (page 41) or
   10 slices Food for Life or Whole Foods
   bread or other gluten-free bread
4 large eggs

1 cup milk (cow, rice, soy)
½ teaspoon vanilla extract
⅛ teaspoon salt

1. If using French bread, cut into ten ½-inch slices. Set aside.

2. In shallow bowl or pie plate, whisk together eggs, milk, vanilla, and salt until thoroughly blended.

3. Dip both sides of each slice into egg-milk mixture. Cook both sides on lightly oiled, preheated griddle or skillet at low-medium temperature until browned. Keep fried slices warm in 250°F oven until serving time. Makes 10 slices. Serves 5 (2 slices each).

4. Serve warm with maple syrup, jam, or jelly.

Calories 205; Fat 9g; Protein 6g; Carbohydrates 24g; Sodium 149mg; Cholesterol 94mg; Fiber 1g

∝• Granola •∞

This makes a small recipe, but one that fits nicely in a fairly thin layer on a 15 x 10-inch jelly roll pan. You can vary the dried fruit as you wish in this morning treat—try dried blueberries, dried peaches, or dried bananas. For a sweeter granola, increase honey to 1/3 to 1/2 cup.

2 cups gluten-free rolled oats*
½ cup shredded coconut flakes
¼ cup sesame seeds
¼ cup sunflower seeds
¼ cup pumpkin seeds
¼ cup almond slivers
½ teaspoon ground cinnamon
¼ teaspoon ground nutmeg
¼ teaspoon salt

¼ cup hot (120°F) water
¼ cup honey or maple syrup
¼ cup brown sugar
1 tablespoon canola oil
2 teaspoons vanilla extract
¼ cup golden raisins
¼ cup dried sweetened cranberries
¼ cup chopped dried apricots

1. Grease 15 x 11-inch baking sheet or line with parchment paper.

2. In large mixing bowl, combine rolled oats through salt.

3. In another bowl, mix together hot water, honey, sugar, oil, and vanilla. Add mixture to dry ingredients. Spread well in pan.

4. Bake 50 to 60 minutes at 300°F, or until lightly browned. Stir every 15 minutes to assure even browning. Watch carefully to avoid burning. Remove from oven and cool 15 minutes. Add dried fruit. Cool completely. Store in airtight container in a dark, dry place. Makes about 4 cups. Serves 8 (½ cup each).
Calories: 270; Fat 12g; Protein 5g; Carbohydrates 39g; Sodium 95mg; Cholesterol 0mg; Fiber 3g

*Available from www.bobsredmill.com, www.creamhillestates.com, www.giftsofnature.net, www.glutenfreeoats.com, or www.onlyoats.com. Check with your physician to see if these oats for right for you.

ℭ• Scones •ℬ

Although they sound like a delicate pastry served by the English at "High Tea," they're actually quite rugged and surprisingly easy to make.

¼ cup butter/canola oil

½ cup milk (cow, rice, soy)

1 large egg

2 tablespoons sugar

1 ¾ cups Flour Blend (page 41)

½ cup tapioca flour

2 teaspoons xanthan gum

1 ½ teaspoons cream of tartar

¾ teaspoon baking soda

½ teaspoon salt

¼ teaspoon soy lecithin granules

½ cup currants

1. Preheat oven to 425°F. Grease nonstick baking sheet.

2. In food processor, blend butter, milk, and egg together until well mixed. Add sugar, flour blend, tapioca flour, xanthan gum, cream of tartar, baking soda, salt, and soy lecithin. Blend just until mixed. Toss in currants and pulse twice. Dough will be soft.

3. Transfer dough to baking sheet, patting with spatula into 8-inch circle, ¾ -inch thick. Bake 15 to 20 minutes or until deeply browned. For crispier, wedge-shaped pieces, cut into 8 wedges with sharp knife and return to oven for final 5 minutes of baking. Serves 8.

Calories 225; Fat 7g; Protein 3g; Carbohydrates 44g; Cholesterol 43mg; Sodium 280; Fiber 1g

ೞ• Pancakes •ಶಾ

For even lighter pancakes, sift the dry ingredients together before blending.

1 cup Flour Blend (page 41)   1 large egg
2 teaspoons sugar   ⅓ to ½ cup milk (cow, rice, soy)
2 teaspoons baking powder   1 tablespoon canola oil
½ teaspoon baking soda   Additional oil for frying
¼ teaspoon salt

1. Blend all ingredients (use ⅓ cup milk to start) in blender.

2. Let batter sit while preheating skillet or griddle to medium-high.

3. Lightly oil hot skillet. Cook a "test" pancake using scant ¼ cup batter. Ad-just batter if necessary by adding remaining milk, a tablespoon at a time. Cook until tops are bubbly (3 to 5 minutes). Turn and cook until golden brown (2 to 3 minutes). Makes 8 four-inch pancakes. Serves 4 (2 pancakes each).
Calories 95; Fat 3g; Protein 2g; Carbohydrates 15g; Sodium 225mg; Cholesterol 28mg; Fiber <1g

ೞ• Buckwheat Pancakes •ಶಾ

Enjoy the hearty flavor of buckwheat. These pancakes benefit from sifting the flour first.

¾ cup Flour Blend (page 41)   ¼ teaspoon salt
¼ cup buckwheat flour   1 large egg
2 ½ teaspoons sugar   ⅓ to ½ cup milk (cow, rice, soy)
2 teaspoons baking powder   1 tablespoon butter/canola oil
½ teaspoon baking soda   Additional oil for frying

1. Blend all ingredients (use ⅓ cup milk to start) in blender.

2. Let batter sit while preheating skillet or griddle to medium-high.

3. Lightly oil hot skillet. Cook a "test" pancake with scant ¼ cup batter. Adjust batter if necessary by adding remaining milk, a tablespoon at a time. Cook until tops are bubbly (3-5 minutes). Turn; cook until golden brown (2-3 minutes). Makes 8 four-inch pancakes. Serves 4 (2 pancakes each).
Calories 245; Fat 6g; Protein 5g; Carbohydrates 47g; Sodium 430mg; Cholesterol 47mg; Fiber 1g

⊱• Waffles •⊰

Prepare your waffle iron (regular or Belgian) following manufacturer's directions. The dimensions and number of waffles will vary depending on your particular appliance.

2 cups Flour Blend (page 41)
¾ cup milk (cow, rice, soy)
4 teaspoons baking powder
2 teaspoons sugar

1 teaspoon baking soda
½ teaspoon salt
2 large eggs, beaten
¼ cup butter/canola oil

1. Whisk all ingredients together in medium bowl.

2. Pour ¼ of batter (or manufacturer's recommended amount) onto heated waffle iron. Close and bake until steaming stops and waffle is deeply browned, about 4 to 6 minutes. Repeat with remaining batter. Makes 4 waffles, 8 inches each. Serves 4 (1 waffle each).

Calories 155; Fat 9g; Protein 3g; Carbohydrates 16g; Sodium 237mg; Cholesterol 55mg; Fiber <1g

ৎ• Desserts •৪৩

Dessert lovers can rejoice! There's something here for every sweet tooth!

Cakes

Apple Spice Cake 125
Basic Cake 113
Boston Cream Pie 116
Carrot Cake 119
Chocolate Cake 121
Chocolate Chip Almond Cake 122
Chocolate Raspberry Cake 123
Coconut Cake 114
Flourless Basic Cake 126
Flourless Chocolate Cake 127
Gingerbread 128
Lemon Cake 117

Pear Upside Down Spice Cake 129
Pineapple Upside-Down Cake 115
Rum Cake 118
Spice Bundt Cake 124

Frosting
Basic Powdered Sugar Frosting 120
Chocolate Glaze 120
Chocolate Powdered Sugar Frosting 120
Cream Cheese Frosting 120
Fluffy White Cooked Frosting 120
Rum Cake Glaze 120

Bars and Cookies

Almond Meringues 132
Basic Drop Cookie 136
Chocolate Meringues 132
Chocolate Brownies 147
Chocolate Cookies 137
Chocolate Chip Cookies 138
Coconut Macaroons 141
Crispy Rice Bars 151
Double Chocolate Cookies 131
Double Chocolate Nut Brownies 148

Gingerbread Cookies 142
Lemon Bars 149
Mexican Wedding Cakes 134
Old-Fashioned Oatmeal Cookies 144
Nutty Oatmeal Cookies 145
Peanut Butter Cookies 146
Seven Layer Bars 150
Spice Drop Cookies 150
Sugar Cut-Out Cookies 133
Whoopies 143

(more desserts on the next page)

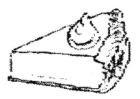

For more delicious desserts:

Wheat-Free Recipes & Menus: Delicious, Healthful Eating for People with Food Sensitivities by Carol Fenster, Ph.D.
Cooking Free: 200 Flavorful Recipes for People with Food Allergies & Multiple Food Sensitivities by Carol Fenster, Ph.D.
Gluten-Free Quick & Easy--From Prep to Plate without the Fuss by Carol Fenster, Ph.D.
1,000 Gluten-Free Recipes by Carol Fenster, Ph.D.

Pies, Puddings ... and More!

ༀ• Basic Cake •ༀ

Use this versatile recipe plain or use the recipes on the following pages for variations.

½ cup butter/canola oil
1 ¼ cups sugar
2 large eggs
1 tablespoon grated lemon peel
2 cups Flour Blend (page 41)
1 ½ teaspoons xanthan gum
½ teaspoon baking powder

½ teaspoon baking soda
½ teaspoon salt
1 ¼ cups buttermilk or 1 tablespoon
  vinegar plus milk (cow, rice, soy)
  to equal 1 ¼ cups
1 teaspoon vanilla extract

1. Have all ingredients at room temperature. Preheat oven to 325°F. Generously grease 10-cup nonstick Bundt pan.

2. Using electric mixer and large mixer bowl, cream together butter and sugar for 2 minutes on medium speed. Mix in eggs on low speed until blended; then add grated lemon peel. (Mixture may curdle; that's ok.)

3. In medium bowl, sift together flour, xanthan gum, baking powder, baking soda, and salt. Add vanilla to buttermilk. On low speed, beat dry ingredients into butter mixture, alternating with buttermilk, beginning and ending with dry ingredients. Mix just until combined. Spoon batter into prepared pan.

4. Bake 50 to 55 minutes or until top is golden brown and tester inserted into center comes out clean. Cool cake in pan for 5 minutes. Remove from pan and cool thoroughly on rack. Serves 12.

Calories: 250; Fat 9g; Protein 3g; Carbohydrates 40g; Sodium 198mg; Cholesterol 57mg; Fiber <1g

ଓଃ• Coconut Cake •ଈଠ

If you're a coconut lover, you'll love this cake.

½ cup butter/canola oil
1 ¼ cups sugar
2 large eggs
2 cups Flour Blend (page 41)
1 ½ teaspoons xanthan gum
½ teaspoon baking powder
½ teaspoon baking soda

½ teaspoon salt
1 ¼ cups light coconut milk
1 tablespoon fresh lemon juice
1 teaspoon vanilla extract
½ cup sweetened coconut flakes
Fluffy White Cooked Frosting (page 120)

1. Have all ingredients at room temperature. Preheat oven to 325°F Generously grease 10-cup Bundt pan.

2. Using electric mixer and large mixer bowl, cream together butter and sugar for 2 minutes on medium speed. Mix in eggs on low speed until blended; then add grated lemon peel. (Mixture may curdle.)

3. In medium bowl, sift together flour, xanthan gum, baking powder, baking soda, and salt. Add vanilla to buttermilk. On low speed, beat dry ingredients into butter mixture, alternating with buttermilk, beginning and ending with dry ingredients. Mix just until combined. Spoon batter into prepared pan.

4. Bake 50 to 55 minutes or until top is golden brown and tester inserted into center comes out clean. Cool cake in pan for 5 minutes. Remove from pan and cool thoroughly on rack. Frost with Fluffy White Cooked Frosting and sprinkle top with ½ cup flaked sweetened coconut. Serves 12.
Calories 325; Fat, 9g; Protein 3g; Carbohydrates 60g; Sodium 197mg; Cholesterol 56mg; Fiber <1g

෫• Pineapple Upside-Down Cake •ෂ

Use this versatile recipe plain or use the recipes on the following pages for variations.

½ cup butter/canola oil
1 ¼ cups sugar
2 large eggs
1 tablespoon grated lemon peel
2 cups Flour Blend (page 41)
1 ½ teaspoons xanthan gum
½ teaspoon baking powder

½ teaspoon baking soda
½ teaspoon salt
1 ¼ cups buttermilk or 1 tablespoon
  vinegar plus milk (cow, rice, soy) to
  equal 1 ¼ cups
1 teaspoon vanilla extract

Topping

½ cup packed light brown sugar

Two cans (14.5 ounces each) pineapple
  slices

1. Have all ingredients at room temperature. Preheat oven to 325ºF Generously grease two 10-inch nonstick pans. Sprinkle with brown sugar. Arrange pineapple slices evenly over sugar. Set aside.

2. Using electric mixer and large mixer bowl, cream together butter and sugar for 2 minutes on medium speed. Mix in eggs on low speed until blended; then add grated lemon peel. (Mixture may curdle.)

3. In medium bowl, sift together flour, xanthan gum, baking powder, baking soda, and salt. Add vanilla to buttermilk. On low speed, beat dry ingredients into butter mixture, alternating with buttermilk, beginning and ending with dry ingredients. Mix just until combined. Spoon batter on pineapple slices in prepared pans .

4. Bake 50 to 55 minutes or until top is golden brown and tester inserted into center comes out clean. Cool cakes in pans 5 minutes. Remove from pan and cool thoroughly on rack. Makes two cakes. Serves 12 (6 slices per cake).
Calories 325; Fat 9g; Protein 3g; Carbohydrates 60g; Sodium 197mg; Cholesterol 56mg; Fiber <1g

☙• Boston Cream Pie •❧

Despite its name, this is not a pie but a double-layer cake with a custard filling and chocolate frosting.

Cake
½ cup butter/canola oil
1 ¼ cups sugar
2 large eggs
1 tablespoon grated lemon peel
2 cups Flour Blend (page 41)
1 ½ teaspoons xanthan gum
½ teaspoon baking powder
½ teaspoon baking soda

½ teaspoon salt
1 ¼ cups buttermilk or 1 tablespoon vinegar
    plus enough milk (cow, rice, soy) to make
    1 ¼ cups
1 teaspoon vanilla extract

Filling and Frosting
½ recipe of Vanilla Pudding (page 157)
½ cup Chocolate Frosting (page 120)

1. Have all ingredients at room temperature. Preheat oven to 325ºF Generously grease two 8-inch pans, lined with waxed paper or parchment paper for easy removal. Set aside.

2. Using electric mixer and large mixer bowl, cream together butter and sugar for 2 minutes on medium speed. Mix in eggs on low speed until blended; then add grated lemon peel. (Mixture may curdle; that's ok.)

3. In medium bowl, sift together flour, xanthan gum, baking powder, baking soda, and salt. Add vanilla to buttermilk. On low speed, beat dry ingredients into butter mixture, alternating with buttermilk, beginning and ending with dry ingredients. Mix just until combined. Spoon batter into prepared pans.

4. Bake 50 to 55 minutes or until top is golden brown and tester inserted into center comes out clean. Cool cake in pan for 5 minutes. Remove from pan and cool thoroughly on rack. Spread one cake layer with Vanilla Pudding. Place remaining layer on top of pudding. Spread Chocolate Frosting on top cake layer. Serve immediately or chill. Serves 12.

Calories 340; Fat 13g; Protein 3g; Carbohydrates 55g; Sodium 218mg; Cholesterol 41mg; Fiber <1g

෪• Lemon Cake • න

Citrus lovers will especially appreciate this delectable cake.

½ cup butter/canola oil
1 ¼ cups sugar
2 large eggs
2 tablespoons grated lemon peel
2 cups Flour Blend (page 41)
1 ½ teaspoons xanthan gum
½ teaspoon baking powder

½ teaspoon baking soda
½ teaspoon salt
1 ¼ cups buttermilk or 1 tablespoon
  vinegar plus milk (cow, rice, soy)
  to equal 1 ¼ cups
1 teaspoon vanilla extract

1. Have all ingredients at room temperature. Preheat oven to 325°F. Generously grease 10-cup nonstick Bundt pan.

2. Using electric mixer and large mixer bowl, cream together butter and sugar for 2 minutes on medium speed. Mix in eggs on low speed until blended; then add grated lemon peel. (Mixture may curdle; that's ok.)

3. In medium bowl, sift together flour, xanthan gum, baking powder, baking soda, and salt. Add vanilla to buttermilk. On low speed, beat dry ingredients into butter mixture, alternating with buttermilk, beginning and ending with dry ingredients. Mix just until combined. Spoon batter into prepared pan.

4. Bake 50 to 55 minutes or until top is golden brown and tester inserted into center comes out clean. Cool cake in pan for 5 minutes. Remove from pan and cool thoroughly on rack. Serves 12.

Calories: 250; Fat 9g; Protein 3g; Carbohydrates 40g; Sodium 198mg; Cholesterol 57mg; Fiber <1g

ೞ• Rum Cake •ജ

Use this versatile recipe plain or use the recipes on the following pages for variations.

½ cup butter/canola oil
1 ¼ cups sugar
2 large eggs
1 tablespoon grated lemon peel
2 cups Flour Blend (page 41)
1 ½ teaspoons xanthan gum
½ teaspoon baking powder

½ teaspoon baking soda
½ teaspoon salt
1 cup buttermilk or 1 tablespoon
  vinegar plus milk (cow, rice, soy)
  to equal 1 ¼ cups
¼ cup light rum
1 teaspoon vanilla extract

1. Have all ingredients at room temperature. Preheat oven to 325°F. Generously grease 10-cup nonstick Bundt pan.

2. Using electric mixer and large mixer bowl, cream together butter and sugar for 2 minutes on medium speed. Mix in eggs on low speed until blended; then add grated lemon peel. (Mixture may curdle.)

3. In medium bowl, sift together flour, xanthan gum, baking powder, baking soda, and salt. Add vanilla to buttermilk. On low speed, beat dry ingredients into butter mixture, alternating with buttermilk, beginning and ending with dry ingredients. Mix just until combined. Spoon batter into prepared pan.

4. Bake 50 to 55 minutes or until top is golden brown and tester inserted into center comes out clean. Cool cake in pan 5 minutes. Remove from pan and cool thoroughly on rack. If desired, brush cake with Rum Cake Glaze (page 120). Then drizzle the cake with Basic Frosting (page 120) using light rum rather than milk as the liquid. Serves 12.

Cake only
Calories 320; Fat 12g; Protein 3g; Carbohydrates 52g; Sodium 202mg; Cholesterol 65mg; Fiber <1g

⊛• Carrot Cake •⊛

This makes a very moist, tender cake that's great with cream cheese frosting.

2 ½ cups Flour Blend (page 41)
2 teaspoons xanthan gum
1 ½ teaspoons baking soda
1 ½ teaspoons baking powder
2 teaspoons cinnamon
1 teaspoon salt
½ teaspoon ground ginger
3 large eggs
2 cups sugar

⅓ cup canola oil
1 cup plain yogurt or ¾ cup milk
  (cow, rice, soy)
1 tablespoon vanilla extract
3 cups finely shredded carrots
1 cup sweetened shredded coconut
1 cup walnuts, chopped
Cream Cheese Frosting (next page)

1. Preheat oven to 350°F. Generously grease 10-cup nonstick Bundt pan. Combine flour blend through ginger in small bowl.

2. In large mixer bowl, beat together eggs, sugar, oil, yogurt, and vanilla extract. Add flour mixture slowly until just blended. Stir in carrots, coconut, and nuts.

3. Pour batter into prepared pan. Bake 45 to 50 minutes or until tester inserted in center of cake comes out clean. Cool on wire rack. Frost. Serves 12.

Cake with Cream Cheese Frosting:
Calories 575; Fat 20g, Protein 6g; Carbohydrates 95g; Sodium 464mg; Cholesterol 62mg; Fiber 3g

Basic Powdered Sugar Frosting*:* In medium bowl, mix 2 cups powdered sugar, ½ teaspoon vanilla extract, ¼ cup softened butter or margarine, and ⅛ teaspoon salt. Add 2 tablespoons milk or substitute and beat with spatula until smooth. For stiffer frosting, add powdered sugar—1 tablespoon at a time. For softer frosting, add milk or water—1 tablespoon at a time.
Per tablespoon:
Calories 110; Fat 4g; Protein <1g; Carbohydrates 20g; Sodium 26mg; Cholesterol 11mg; Fiber 0g

Chocolate Powdered Sugar Frosting*:* Add 2 tablespoons cocoa to Basic Powdered Sugar Frosting.
Calories 110; Fat 4g; Protein <1g; Carbohydrates 20g; Sodium 26mg; Cholesterol 11mg; Fiber 0g

Chocolate Glaze: In 2-cup glass measure, combine 3 tablespoons cocoa, 1 tablespoon butter or margarine, and ⅓ cup corn syrup. Microwave on high 1 ½ to 2 minutes until smooth, stirring twice during cooking. Immediately pour over cooled cake, allowing glaze to run down sides. Cool 30 minutes before serving. Makes ½ cup.
Per tablespoon:
Calories 5; Fat 2g; Protein <1g; Carbohydrates 12g; Sodium 17mg; Cholesterol 4mg; Fiber <1g

Cream Cheese Frosting: Beat together softened package (3 ounces) cream cheese (cow, soy), 2 cups powdered sugar, 2 tablespoons milk, and 1 teaspoon vanilla. Serves 12.
Calories 105; Fat 3g; Protein <1g; Carbohydrates 20g; Sodium 23mg; Cholesterol 8mg; Fiber 0g

Fluffy White Cooked Frosting: In double boiler over simmering water, combine 3 large egg whites, 1 ¼ cups granulated sugar, ¼ teaspoon cream of tartar, and 3 tablespoons cold water. Beat 7 minutes with portable electric mixer—or to desired consistency. Remove from heat, stir in 1 teaspoon vanilla extract. Use immediately. Serves 12.
Calories 85; Fat 0g; Protein <1g; Carbohydrates 21g; Sodium 14mg; Cholesterol 0mg; Fiber 0g

Rum Cake Glaze: In 1-quart glass measuring cup, microwave ¼ cup light brown sugar and 3 tablespoons butter or margarine, on high until bubbly (check at 1 minute). Stir twice during cooking. Whisk in 1 tablespoon light rum or lemon juice and ⅓ cup powdered sugar until smooth. Immediately pour over cake. Cool. Serves 8.
Calories 60; Fat 1g; Protein <1g; Carbohydrates 12mg; Sodium 3mg; Cholesterol 4mg; Fiber <1g

ભ• Chocolate Cake •ഇ

Every kitchen needs a good, versatile chocolate cake. Use this one as the base for a variety of chocolate delights. Bake it as cupcakes, layer cakes . . . and more.

⅔ cup butter/canola oil
1 ½ cups brown sugar
2 large eggs
2 teaspoons vanilla extract
½ cup milk (cow, rice, soy)
2 ⅔ cups Flour Blend (page 41)

⅔ cup unsweetened cocoa (not Dutch)
1 ½ teaspoons xanthan gum
1 ½ teaspoons baking soda
½ teaspoon salt
1 cup hot (120°F) brewed coffee

1. Preheat oven to 350°F. Generously grease 10-cup nonstick Bundt pan.

2. Blend butter and sugar in large bowl with electric mixer 2 minutes. Thoroughly mix in eggs, vanilla, and milk.

3. Sift dry ingredients together (flour blend through salt). Add hot coffee alternately with dry ingredients and mix until thoroughly blended.

4. Pour into prepared pan and bake 45 to 50 minutes or until tester inserted in center comes out clean. Serves 12.
Calories: 325; Fat 12g; Protein 4g; Carbohydrates 54g; Sodium 285mg; Cholesterol 64mg; Fiber 3g

Chocolate Raspberry Cake: Reduce coffee or warm water to ¼ cup. Add 1 cup thoroughly crushed raspberries.
Calories 330; Fat 12g; Protein 4g; Carbohydrates 55g; Sodium 285mg; Cholesterol 64mg; Fiber 3g

⚝• Chocolate Chip Almond Cake •⚝

Every family needs a good, versatile chocolate cake. Use this one as the base for a variety of chocolate delights. Bake it as cupcakes, layer cakes . . . and more.

⅔ cup butter/canola oil
1 ½ cups packed light brown sugar
2 large eggs
2 teaspoons vanilla extract
½ cup milk (cow, rice, soy)
2 ⅔ cups Flour Blend (page 41)
⅔ cup unsweetened cocoa (not Dutch)

1 ½ teaspoons xanthan gum
1 ½ teaspoons baking soda
½ teaspoon salt
1 cup hot (120°F) brewed coffee
1 teaspoon almond extract
½ cup gluten-free chocolate chips
½ cup chopped or sliced almonds

1. Preheat oven to 350°F. Generously grease 10-cup nonstick Bundt pan.

2. Blend butter and sugar in large bowl with electric mixer 2 minutes. Thoroughly mix in eggs, vanilla, and milk.

3. Sift dry ingredients together (flour blend through salt). Add hot coffee alternately with dry ingredients and mix until thoroughly blended. Gently stir in chocolate chips and almonds.

4. Pour into prepared pan and bake 45 to 50 minutes or until tester inserted in center comes out clean. Serves 12.

Calories 395; Fat 17g; Protein 5g; Carbohydrates 58g; Sodium 291mg; Cholesterol 65mg; Fiber 3g

∝• Chocolate Raspberry Cake •∞

Raspberries complement chocolate and will leave your guest wondering...what's that wonderful taste?

⅔ cup butter/canola oil
1 ½ cups brown sugar
2 large eggs
2 teaspoons vanilla extract
½ cup milk (cow, rice, soy)
2 ⅔ cups Flour Blend (page 41)

⅔ cup unsweetened cocoa (not Dutch)
1 ½ teaspoons xanthan gum
1 ½ teaspoons baking soda
½ teaspoon salt
¼ cup hot (120°F) brewed coffee
1 cup crushed fresh raspberries

1. Preheat oven to 350°F. Generously grease 10-cup nonstick Bundt pan.

2. Blend butter and sugar in large bowl with electric mixer 2 minutes. Thoroughly mix in eggs, vanilla, and milk.

3. Sift dry ingredients together (flour blend through salt). Add hot coffee alternately with dry ingredients and mix until thoroughly blended. Stir in crushed raspberries.

4. Pour into prepared pan and bake 45 to 50 minutes or until tester inserted in center comes out clean. Serves 12.

Calories 330; Fat 12g; Protein 4g; Carbohydrates 55g; Sodium 285mg; Cholesterol 64mg; Fiber 3g

❀ Spice Bundt Cake ❀

This intensely flavored spice cake continues to be one of my most popular recipes.

3 cups Flour Blend (page 41)
2 teaspoons xanthan gum
1 ½ teaspoons baking soda
1 teaspoon salt
1 ½ tablespoons ground ginger
1 tablespoon ground cinnamon
½ teaspoon ground nutmeg

¼ teaspoon ground cloves
1 ½ cups milk (cow, rice, soy)
2 cups brown sugar, packed
¾ cup butter/canola oil
½ cup molasses
1 ½ teaspoons vanilla extract
2 large eggs, beaten

1. Preheat oven to 325°F. Generously grease 10-cup nonstick Bundt pan.

2. Sift together flours, xanthan gum, baking soda, salt, ginger, cinnamon, nutmeg, and cloves in large mixing bowl.

3. Combine milk and brown sugar in heavy saucepan and bring just to boil over medium heat. Remove from heat and add butter, molasses, and vanilla.

4. When butter is melted, add butter and sugar mixture to flour mixture in mixing bowl and mix until thoroughly blended. Add eggs and mix until blended.

5. Pour batter into prepared pan. Bake 55 to 60 minutes, or until toothpick inserted in center of cake comes out clean. Cool cake in pan for 5 minutes. Invert cake onto rack to finish cooling. Serves 12.

Calories: 422; Fat 14g; Protein 4g; Carbohydrates 74g; Sodium 399mg; Cholesterol 69mg; Fiber 2g

ೲ• Apple Spice Cake •ೞ

This intensely flavored spice cake continues to be one of my most popular recipes.

3 cups Flour Blend (page 41)
2 teaspoons xanthan gum
1 ½ teaspoons baking soda
1 teaspoon salt
1 ½ tablespoons ground ginger
1 tablespoon ground cinnamon
½ teaspoon ground nutmeg
¼ teaspoon ground cloves
1 ½ cups milk (cow, rice, soy)

2 cups brown sugar, packed
¾ cup butter/canola oil
½ cup molasses
1 ½ teaspoon vanilla extract
2 large eggs, beaten
1 cup peeled, grated Granny Smith apples
½ cup chopped walnuts

1. Preheat oven to 325°F. Generously grease 10-cup nonstick Bundt pan.

2. Sift together flours, xanthan gum, baking soda, salt, ginger, cinnamon, nutmeg, and cloves in large mixing bowl.

3. Combine milk and brown sugar in heavy saucepan and bring just to boil over medium heat. Remove from heat and add butter, molasses, and vanilla.

4. When butter is melted, add butter and sugar mixture to flour mixture in mixing bowl and mix until thoroughly blended. Add eggs and mix until blended.

5. Pour batter into prepared pan. Bake 55 to 60 minutes, or until toothpick inserted in center of cake comes out clean. Cool cake in pan for 5 minutes. Invert cake onto rack to finish cooling. Serves 12.

Calories 458; Fat 16g; Protein 4g; Carbohydrates 77g; Sodium 399mg; Cholesterol 69mg; Fiber 2g

෪• Flourless Basic Cake • හ

This cake rises, then falls somewhat for a dense delight. For a lighter texture, separate the eggs and beat the egg whites to soft peaks with your electric mixer. Blend remaining ingredients together; then fold into the egg whites by hand.

2 cups whole or slivered almonds, ground (measured before grinding)
1 cup sugar
½ cup melted butter/canola oil

Grated peel from 1 lemon
4 large eggs
1 teaspoon almond extract
⅛ teaspoon salt

1. Preheat oven to 350°F. Grease 9 or 10-inch springform pan and line with parchment paper.

2. In food processor, blend almonds to consistency of meal.

3. Add remaining ingredients and blend 30-40 seconds. Stop machine, scrape down sides with spatula, and blend again 30-40 seconds. Pour into springform pan.

4. Bake 40 to 45 minutes or until toothpick in center comes out clean. Cool in pan 5 to 10 minutes. Gently run knife around edge of pan to loosen cake. Remove outer rim. Cool completely on wire rack. Gently run knife between pan bottom and cake to loosen; remove parchment. Invert onto serving plate. Serve with a dusting of powdered sugar, your favorite frosting, or glaze top with melted apricot preserves or orange marmalade. Serves 10.

Calories 355; Fat 25g; Protein 8g; Carbohydrates 25g; Sodium 58mg; Cholesterol 110mg; Fiber 3g

---

 Carol's Tip: Vary the flavor of this versatile cake—or any basic cake—by adding ½ teaspoon cinnamon or 1 teaspoon almond extract.

ॐ• Flourless Chocolate Cake •ॐ

This is my "go-to" recipe for company because it's perfect no matter how it turns out. For a lighter texture, separate the eggs and beat the egg whites to soft peaks with your electric mixer. Blend remaining ingredients together; then fold into egg whites by hand.

**2 cups whole pecans (measure before
 grinding)
1 cup packed light brown sugar
1 cup whole eggs (about 4 or 5)**

**½ cup light olive oil
5 tablespoons unsweetened cocoa
1 teaspoon vanilla extract
⅛ teaspoon salt**

1. Preheat oven to 350°F. Grease; then line bottom of 8 or 9-inch spring-form pan with waxed paper or parchment paper.

2. Grind nuts in food processor to meal-like texture.

3. Add remaining ingredients and process 30 to 40 seconds. Scrape down sides of bowl and process another 30 seconds.

4. Transfer batter to prepared pan. Bake 40 to 45 minutes or until toothpick inserted into center comes out clean. Cake rises as it bakes, then falls slightly as it cools. Cool 15 minutes in pan on wire rack. Cut around edge to loosen cake from pan edges. Release pan sides; remove paper liner. Slice into 10 pieces. Top with your favorite frosting, glaze with melted chocolate, or dust with powdered sugar. Serves 10 (small slices).

Calories: 385; Fat 31g; Protein 5g; Carbohydrates 27g; Sodium 64mg; Cholesterol 86mg; Fiber 3g

 Carol's Tip: For best results, use the best quality cocoa you can afford.

ℭℰ• Gingerbread •℔

The aroma of this gingerbread while it bakes is just heavenly.

Cake

¼ cup canola oil
½ cup packed light brown sugar
1 large egg
½ cup molasses
1 teaspoon vanilla extract
1 ½ cups Flour Blend (page 41)
1 teaspoon baking soda

1 ½ teaspoons ground ginger
¾ teaspoon cinnamon
½ teaspoon cloves
½ teaspoon salt
½ cup buttermilk or 1 teaspoon vinegar
  plus enough milk (cow, rice, soy)
  to make ½ cup

Lemon Sauce

¼ cup sugar
1 tablespoon cornstarch
⅛ teaspoon salt
½ cup water

2 teaspoons grated lemon peel
1 tablespoon lemon juice
1 teaspoon canola oil

1. Preheat oven to 350°F. In a large bowl, beat oil and brown sugar with electric mixer until well blended. Add egg, molasses, and vanilla. Beat well. Mix flour with baking soda, ginger, cinnamon, cloves, and salt. Add flour mixture alternately with buttermilk to creamed mixture. Pour into greased 8 or 9-inch round or square nonstick pan.

2. Bake 30 minutes or until toothpick inserted into center comes out clean. Cool pan on wire rack. Drizzle with lemon sauce (see below) before serving. Serves 12.

Lemon Sauce: In small pan, combine sugar, cornstarch, and salt. Gradually stir in ½ cup water. Cook and stir over medium heat until mixture thickens. Stir in lemon peel, lemon juice, and oil.

Calories 200; Fat 6g; Protein 2g; Carbohydrates 37g; Cholesterol 18mg; Sodium 250mg; Fiber<1g

ℭℨ• Pear Upside-Down Spice Cake •ℬ℧

The aroma of this gingerbread while it bakes is just heavenly. It is a great winter dessert when pears are in season.

Cake

¼ cup canola oil
½ cup brown sugar, packed
1 large egg
½ cup molasses
1 teaspoon vanilla extract
1 ½ cups Flour Blend (page 41)
1 teaspoon baking soda

1 ½ teaspoons ground ginger
¾ teaspoon cinnamon
½ teaspoon cloves
½ teaspoon salt
½ cup buttermilk or 1 teaspoon vinegar
    plus enough milk (cow, rice, soy) to
    make ½ cup

Topping

¾ cup packed light brown sugar   1 firm, ripe cored pear cut into 16 thin
                                       wedges

1. Preheat oven to 350°F. Generously grease 10-inch plate. Sprinkle with brown sugar and layer pear slices evenly over sugar in decorative pinwheel design.

2. In large bowl, cream oil and brown sugar with electric mixer. Add egg, molasses, and vanilla. Beat well. Mix flour with baking soda, ginger, cinnamon, cloves, and salt. Add flour mixture alternately with buttermilk to creamed mixture. Pour batter on top of pears and brown sugar in prepared pan.

3. Bake 30 minutes or until toothpick inserted into center comes out clean. Cool pan on wire rack. Drizzle with lemon sauce (see below) before serving. Serves 12.
Calories 245; Fat 6g; Protein 2g; Carbohydrates 48g; Sodium 232mg; Cholesterol 18mg; Fiber 1g

❦ Bread Pudding ❧

Use the Basic Bread in this book. Or, for a delightful change, try using Banana Bread or other quick breads instead. Or, use a neutrally-flavored bread made by Whole Foods.

Bread Pudding
6 cups gluten-free bread cubes
2 cups milk
½ cup sugar
4 large eggs
1 teaspoon grated lemon peel
1 teaspoon vanilla extract
1 teaspoon lemon extract
1 cup fresh blueberries

Sauce
1 cup half-and-half or ¾ cup whole
   milk (cow, rice, soy)
3 large egg yolks
2 tablespoons sugar
1 teaspoon cornstarch
¼ cup honey
1 teaspoon vanilla extract

Bread Pudding

1. Preheat oven to 325°F. Grease 8-inch nonstick square baking dish.

2. Whisk together milk, sugar, 4 eggs, lemon peel, and vanilla and lemon extracts.

3. Place half of cubed bread on bottom of dish. Top with blueberries and half of the egg mixture. Top with remaining bread, then remaining egg mixture. Let stand 15 minutes, occasionally pressing down on bread.

4. Bake until top begins to brown, about 45 minutes to 1 hour.

Sauce
Bring half-and-half to simmer in heavy pan. Whisk together egg yolks, sugar, and cornstarch in medium-sized bowl. Gradually whisk in hot half-and-half. Return mixture to heavy pan and stir over low-medium heat until mixture thickens and leaves path on back of spoon when finger is drawn across, about 3 minutes. Do not boil. Mix in honey and vanilla. Serve on pudding. Serves 6.
Calories 430; Fat 16g; Protein 11g; Carbohydrates 61g; Sodium 132mg; Cholesterol 275mg; Fiber 2g

෨• Cream Puffs •෨

Use versatile Cream Puffs as dessert or fill with savory fillings for lunch.

½ cup white rice flour
¼ cup potato starch
¾ cup water
5 tablespoons butter/canola oil
2 teaspoons sugar
¼ teaspoon salt

3 large eggs (room temperature)
½ cup whipping cream, whipped to
    stiff peaks or use 1 ½ cups non-dairy
    topping
1 tablespoon sugar
Powdered sugar for garnish

1. Grease baking sheet or line with parchment paper. Preheat oven to 450°F. Mix rice flour and potato starch together and set aside.

2. Bring water, butter, sugar, and salt to a boil in medium saucepan over medium-high heat. Immediately remove from heat and stir in flour, all at once. Return to heat and continue stirring until mixture pulls away from sides of pan and film forms on pan bottom.

3. Remove from heat; transfer to mixing bowl. Beat in eggs, one at a time—beating with electric mixer after each addition until smooth before adding next egg. Or, use food processor.

4. Drop a dozen 2-inch mounds of dough onto baking sheet with spring-action ice cream scoop.

5. Bake 20 minutes, then reduce oven temperature to 350°F and continue baking another 15 minutes—or until cream puffs are deep golden brown. Remove from oven. Immediately cut 1-inch horizontal slit in side of cream puff, right where you'll eventually cut them completely in half. Cool on wire racks. When cool, cut completely in half horizontally along slit and fill with whipped cream or desired filling. Makes 12. Serves 12. (1 Cream Puff each.)

Calories 135; Fat 10g; Protein 2g; Carbohydrates 10g; Sodium 68mg; Cholesterol 80mg; Fiber <1g

ෙ෩· Almond Meringues ·෩ඏ

These little delicacies are amazingly simple.

4 egg whites (room temperature) **½ cup powdered sugar**
¼ teaspoon cream of tartar **1 teaspoon almond extract**

1. Preheat oven to 225°F. Line baking sheet with parchment paper.

2. Beat egg whites until foamy. Add cream of tartar and beat to soft peaks. Add powdered sugar gradually—2 tablespoons at a time—while beating to very stiff peaks. Stir in almond extract.

3. Drop 24 dollops onto baking sheet, leaving 1 inch between cookies.

4. Bake 2 hours or until cookies are firm and crisp. Turn baking sheet after 1 hour for more even baking. Cool on wire rack. For maximum crispness, cool in oven with door closed. Store in airtight container. Makes 24 cookies.
Calories 15; Fat 0g; Protein <1g; Carbohydrates 3g; Sodium 9mg; Cholesterol 0mg; Fiber 0g

Chocolate Meringues: Omit almond extract. Replace 1 tablespoon of powdered sugar with 1 tablespoon Dutch (European-style or alkali) cocoa powder.
Calories 13; Fat <1g,; Protein <1g; Carbohydrates 2g; Sodium 9mg; Cholesterol 0mg; Fiber <1g

ೞ• Sugar Cut-Out Cookies •ಐ

This recipe works great for baking cut-out cookie for the holidays.

¼ cup butter/buttery spread
2 tablespoons honey
½ cup sugar
1 tablespoon vanilla extract
2 teaspoons grated lemon peel
1 ½ cups Flour Blend (page 41)

1 teaspoon xanthan gum
½ teaspoon salt
1 teaspoon baking powder
½ teaspoon baking soda
2 tablespoons water (if needed)
Additional rice flour for rolling

1. In food processor, combine butter (room temperature, not melted), honey, sugar, vanilla, and lemon peel. Process 1 minute. Add dry ingredients and blend until mixture forms large clumps. Scrape down sides or bowl with spatula and blend until mixture forms ball again. Add water only if necessary—1 tablespoon at a time. Shape into flat disk; refrigerate 2 hours.

2. Preheat oven to 325°F. Using half of dough, roll to ¼-inch thickness between sheets of plastic wrap which are sprinkled with rice flour. Keep remaining dough chilled until ready to use. Cut into desired shapes (about 2 inches in diameter) and transfer to baking sheet that is lightly greased or lined with parchment paper or non-stick baking liners. Repeat with remaining dough.

3. Bake 10 to 12 minutes or until cookies are lightly browned. Cool 5 minutes on baking sheet. Remove from baking sheet and cool on wire rack. Makes 16.

Calories 100; Fat 3g; Protein <1g; Carbohydrates 18g; Sodium 127mg; Cholesterol 8mg; Fiber <1g

℀• Mexican Wedding Cakes •℁

I'm not sure where these delectable little morsels got their name, but they are certainly delicious.

¼ cup butter/buttery spread
2 tablespoons honey
½ cup sugar
1 tablespoon vanilla extract
2 teaspoons grated lemon peel
1 ½ cups Flour Blend (page 41)
1 teaspoon xanthan gum

½ teaspoon salt
1 teaspoon baking powder
½ teaspoon baking soda
2 tablespoons water (if needed)
Additional rice flour for rolling
¼ cup powdered sugar (for rolling)

1. In food processor, combine butter (room temperature, not melted), honey, sugar, vanilla, and lemon peel. Process 1 minute. Add dry ingredients and blend until mixture forms large clumps. Scrape down sides or bowl with spatula and blend until mixture forms ball again. Add water only if necessary—1 tablespoon at a time. Shape into flat disk; refrigerate 2 hours.

2. Preheat oven to 325°F. Form chilled dough into 32 one-inch balls. Roll in ¼ cup powdered sugar; chill again 1 hour. Place on baking sheet that is lightly greased or lined with parchment paper. Bake 10 to 12 minutes or until set. Cool 5 minutes on sheet, then on wire rack. Serves 16 (2 cookies each).
Calories 54; Fat 2g Protein <1g; Carbohydrates 10g; Sodium 64mg; Cholesterol 4mg; Fiber <1g

Tips for Successful "Cut-Out" Cookies

1. To avoid sticking, use non-stick baking liners (such as Silpat®) or parchment paper.

2. Insulated baking sheets assure even baking and won't buckle.

3. Metal cookie cutters work better than plastic cookie cutters.

4. If the chilled dough is too stiff, leave dough at room temperature 15 to 20 minutes. Or, knead with hands to make dough more pliable. If dough is too soft after rolling, chill or freeze until firm—then cut into desired shapes. Do not roll dough thinner than ¼ inch.

5. If you're having trouble transferring the cookies to the baking sheet, try rolling the dough onto parchment paper or nonstick liners, cut desired shapes, remove scraps of dough (leaving cut-out cookies on paper) and transfer paper or liner (cookies and all) to baking sheet.

6. Chill shaped cookies 30 minutes before baking.

7. Cookies will brown much faster on a gray nonstick cookie sheet than they will on a light-colored shiny cookie sheet. For cookies that brown too quickly, try using the light-colored shiny cookie sheet rather than the gray nonstick type. Lining the sheet with parchment paper will help reduce excessive browning.

↶• Basic Drop Cookies •↷

This dough makes a variety of great cookies. Don't melt the butter or margarine.

1 ½ cups Flour Blend (page 41)	¾ cup packed light brown sugar
1 teaspoon xanthan gum	⅓ cup granulated sugar
½ teaspoon baking soda	2 teaspoons vanilla extract
¼ teaspoon salt	1 extra large egg
¼ cup butter/buttery spread (not diet)	

1. Preheat oven to 350°F. Mix together flour blend, xanthan gum, baking soda, and salt. Set aside. Generously grease 13 x 9-inch baking sheet or line with parchment paper.

2. In large mixer bowl, combine remaining ingredients. Beat in flour mixture on low speed, mixing thoroughly. Remove dough from bowl, wrap tightly, and chill for 30 minutes. Drop by tablespoonfuls (or ice cream scoop) on baking sheet.

3. Bake 10 to 12 minutes in center rack of oven or until browned. Cool 2 to 3 minutes before removing from cookie sheet. Makes 24.

Calories: 85; Fat 2g; Protein <1g; Carbohydrates 16g; Sodium 31mg; Cholesterol 16mg; Fiber <1g

Carol's Tip: For refrigerator cookies, pat dough into 1-inch diameter roll on cutting board. Cut in 1-inch slices; then lay slices flat on cutting board. Wrap cutting board tightly and freeze. Remove cookie slices from cutting board and put in plastic recloseable freezer bag. To bake, place frozen slices of cookie dough flat side down on baking sheet and bake as directed, allowing extra time for baking.

☙ Chocolate Cookies ❧

This dough makes a variety of great cookies. Don't melt the butter.

1 ½ cups Flour Blend (page 41)
2 tablespoons unsweetened cocoa, (not Dutch)
1 teaspoon xanthan gum
½ teaspoon baking soda
¼ teaspoon salt

¼ cup butter/buttery spread (not diet)
¾ cup packed light brown sugar
⅓ cup granulated sugar
2 teaspoons vanilla extract
1 extra large egg

1. Preheat oven to 350ºF. Mix together flour blend, xanthan gum, baking soda, and salt. Set aside. Generously grease 13 x 9-inch baking sheet or line with parchment paper.

2. In large mixer bowl, combine remaining ingredients. Beat in flour mixture on low speed, mixing thoroughly. Remove dough from bowl, wrap tightly, and chill for 30 minutes. Drop by tablespoonfuls (or ice cream scoop) on baking sheet.

3. Bake 10 to 12 minutes in center rack of oven or until browned. Cool 2 to 3 minutes before removing from cookie sheet. Makes 24.

Calories: 85; Fat 2g; Protein <1g; Carbohydrates 16g; Sodium 31mg; Cholesterol 16mg; Fiber <1g

⚛• Chocolate Chip Cookies •⚛

This dough makes a variety of great cookies. Don't melt the butter or margarine.

1 ½ cups Flour Blend (page 41)
1 teaspoon xanthan gum
½ teaspoon baking soda
¼ teaspoon salt
¼ cup cold butter/buttery spread (not
   diet) or shortening

¾ cup packed light brown sugar
⅓ cup granulated sugar
2 teaspoons vanilla extract
1 extra large egg
1 cup gluten-free chocolate chips
¼ cup chopped walnuts

1. Preheat oven to 350ºF. Generously grease 13 x 9-inch baking sheet or line with parchment paper. Mix together flour blend, xanthan gum, baking soda, and salt. Set aside.

2. In large mixer bowl, beat butter until smooth. Add sugars, vanilla, and egg and blend thoroughly. Beat in flour mixture on low speed, mixing thoroughly. Remove dough from bowl, wrap tightly, and chill for 1 hour. Drop by tablespoonfuls (or ice cream scoops) on baking sheet.

3. Bake 10 to 12 minutes in center rack of oven or until browned. Cool 2 to 3 minutes before removing from cookie sheet. Makes 24.

Calories 130; Fat 5g; Protein 1g; Carbohydrates 21g; Sodium 37mg; Cholesterol 17mg; Fiber <!g

○§• Double Chocolate Cookies •※○

This dough makes a variety of great cookies. Don't melt the butter or margarine.

1 ½ cups Flour Blend (page 41)
2 tablespoons unsweetened natural cocoa (not Dutch)
1 teaspoon xanthan gum
½ teaspoon baking soda
¼ teaspoon salt
¼ cup butter/buttery spread (not diet) or shortening

¾ cup packed light brown sugar
⅓ cup granulated sugar
2 teaspoons vanilla extract
1 extra large egg
1 cup gluten-free chocolate chips
¼ cup chopped walnuts

1. Preheat oven to 350°F. Mix together flour blend, xanthan gum, baking soda, and salt. Set aside. Generously grease 13 x 9-inch baking sheet or line with parchment paper.

2. In large mixer bowl, combine remaining ingredients. Beat in flour mixture on low speed, mixing thoroughly. Remove dough from bowl, wrap tightly, and chill for 30 minutes. Drop by tablespoonfuls (or ice cream scoop) on baking sheet.

3. Bake 10 to 12 minutes in center rack of oven or just until they firm up. Cool 2 to 3 minutes before removing from cookie sheet. Makes 24.
Calories 130; Fat 5g, Protein 1g; Carbohydrates 21g; Sodium 37mg; Cholesterol 17mg; Fiber <!g

☞ Spice Drop Cookies ☜

This dough makes a variety of great cookies. Don't melt the butter or margarine.

1 ½ cups Flour Blend (page 41)
1 teaspoon xanthan gum
½ teaspoon baking soda
¼ teaspoon salt
¼ cup butter/buttery spread (not diet) or shortening
¾ cup packed light brown sugar

⅓ cup granulated sugar
½ teaspoon cinnamon
¼ teaspoon ground nutmeg
⅛ teaspoon ground cloves
2 teaspoons vanilla extract
1 extra large egg

1. Preheat oven to 350°F. Mix together flour blend, xanthan gum, baking soda, and salt. Set aside. Generously grease 13 x 9-inch baking sheet or line with parchment paper.

2. In large mixer bowl, combine remaining ingredients. Beat in flour mixture on low speed, mixing thoroughly. Remove dough from bowl, wrap tightly, and chill for 1 hour. Drop by tablespoonfuls (or use ice cream scoop) on baking sheet.

3. Bake 10 to 12 minutes in center rack of oven or until browned. Cool 2 to 3 minutes before removing from cookie sheet. Makes 24.

Calories: 85; Fat 2g; Protein <1g; Carbohydrates 16g; Sodium 31mg; Cholesterol 16mg; Fiber <1g

❦ Coconut Macaroons ❧

These are so moist and delicious—you can't stop with just one! Drizzle a little chocolate on these for even greater decadence. Either shredded or flaked coconut will work.

Dry Ingredients
1 package (14 ounces) sweetened shredded
  coconut
1 cup powdered sugar
½ cup cornstarch
1 teaspoon xanthan gum
⅛ teaspoon salt

Wet Ingredients
3 egg whites
1 teaspoon vanilla extract

1. Preheat oven to 350°F. Grease large baking sheet or line with parchment paper. Set aside.

2. Combine all dry ingredients in food processor and pulse just until blended. Add egg whites and vanilla. Blend until completely mixed. Dough will be stiff.

3. With wet hands, form 15 balls—1 ½-inches in diameter—on baking sheet. Leave at least 1 inch between cookies.

4. Bake 15 to 20 minutes or until cookies start to brown around edges. Remove from oven and cool on baking sheet 10 minutes. Transfer to wire rack and cool completely. Store in tightly closed container. Makes 15.
Calories 185; Fat 9g; Protein 1g; Carbohydrates 25g; Sodium 100mg; Cholesterol 0mg; Fiber 1g

ᥡ• Gingerbread Cookies •ᥣ

These cookies produce a heavenly aroma as they bake! Bet you can't eat just one!

¼ cup butter/buttery spread (not diet)
3 tablespoons molasses
½ cup packed light brown sugar
1 teaspoon vanilla extract
1 ¼ cups Flour Blend (page 41)
1 teaspoon xanthan gum
½ teaspoon salt

1 teaspoon baking soda
1 ½ teaspoons ground cinnamon
1 ½ teaspoons ground ginger
¼ teaspoon ground nutmeg
¼ teaspoon ground cloves
2 tablespoons water (if needed)

1. In food processor, combine butter (room temperature), molasses, sugar, and vanilla. Add remaining ingredients. Blend until thoroughly mixed together and dough forms ball. (Add water, 1 tablespoon at a time, only if mixture fails to form large ball—or if using electric mixer instead of food processor.) Shape dough into 1-inch flat disk; cover and refrigerate 1 hour.

2. Preheat oven to 325°F. Grease baking sheet or line with parchment paper. Set aside.

3. Shape dough into 1-inch balls and place on baking sheet. Flatten slightly with bottom of drinking glass.

4. Bake 20 to 25 minutes on middle rack, or until cookies start to brown on the bottom. Cool cookies on sheet for 5 minutes, then transfer to wire rack to cool. Store in airtight container. Makes 16.
Calories 98g; Fat 3g; Protein <1g; Carbohydrates 18g; Sodium 156mg; Cholesterol 8mg; Fiber <1g

ᚳᚱ• Whoopies •ᛊᚩ

These cookies produce a heavenly aroma as they bake! And the kids will love assembling the cookies themselves. Bet you can't eat just one!

¼ cup butter/buttery spread (not diet)
3 tablespoons molasses
½ cup packed light brown sugar
1 teaspoon vanilla extract
1 ¼ cups Flour Blend (page 41)
1 teaspoon xanthan gum
½ teaspoon salt

1 teaspoon baking soda
1 ½ teaspoons ground cinnamon
1 ½ teaspoons ground ginger
¼ teaspoon ground nutmeg
¼ teaspoon ground cloves
2 tablespoons water (if needed)

Filling

1 cup powdered sugar
¼ cup butter/buttery spread

1 package (3 ounces) cream cheese
  or extra-firm tofu
2 tablespoons marshmallow crème

1. In food processor, combine butter (room temperature), molasses, sugar, and vanilla. Add remaining ingredients. Blend until thoroughly mixed together and dough forms ball. (Add water, 1 tablespoon at a time, only if mixture fails to form large ball—or if using electric mixer instead of food processor.) Shape dough into 1-inch flat disk; cover and refrigerate 1 hour.

2. Preheat oven to 325ºF. Grease baking sheet or line with parchment paper. Set aside.

3. Shape dough into 1-inch balls and place on baking sheet. Flatten slightly with bottom of drinking glass.

4. Bake 20 to 25 minutes on middle rack, or until cookies start to brown on the bottom. Cool cookies on sheet for 5 minutes, then transfer to wire rack to cool. Store in airtight container. Makes 16.

Calories 345; Fat 15g; Protein 2g; Carbohydrates 52g; Sodium 411mg; Cholesterol 28mg; Fiber 1g

෬• Old-Fashioned Oatmeal Cookies •෩

These make hearty cookies, perfect for after-school munching.

1 cup Flour Blend (page 41)
¼ cup potato flour
2 tablespoons tapioca flour
½ cup packed light brown sugar
1 teaspoon xanthan gum
¾ to 1 teaspoon ground cinnamon
½ teaspoon salt
½ teaspoon baking soda

½ teaspoon baking powder
1 large egg
¼ cup butter/buttery spread (not diet)
½ cup applesauce
2 tablespoons molasses
1 teaspoon vanilla extract
⅔ cup gluten-free rolled oats*
¾ cup gluten-free chocolate chips or raisins

1. Preheat oven to 325°F. Lightly grease cookie sheet or line with parchment paper.

2. In food processor, combine egg, butter, applesauce, molasses, and vanilla until well blended. Add dry ingredients and rolled oats to food processor. Pulse until thoroughly mixed. Gently stir in chocolate chips (or raisins). Dough will be somewhat stiff.

3. Drop by tablespoons (or use spring-action ice cream scoop for evenly shaped cookies) onto prepared cookie sheet. Flatten each cookie to ½-inch thickness with wet spatula.

4. Bake 20 to 25 minutes or until edges begin to brown. Cool on baking sheet 5 minutes. Transfer cookies to wire rack to cool completely. Makes 12.

Calories 210; Fat 8g; Protein 2g; Carbohydrates 34g; Sodium 180mg; Cholesterol 30mg; Fiber 1g

*Available from www.bobsredmill.com, www.creamhillestates.com, www.giftsofnature.net, www.glutenfreeoats.com, or www.onlyoats.com. Check with your physician to see if these oats are right for you.

ભ· Nutty Oatmeal Cookies ·ঞ

These make hearty cookies, perfect for after-school munching.

1 cup Flour Blend (page 41)
¼ cup potato flour
2 tablespoons tapioca flour
½ cup packed light brown sugar
1 teaspoon xanthan gum
1 teaspoon cinnamon
½ teaspoon salt
½ teaspoon baking soda
½ teaspoon baking powder
1 large egg

¼ cup butter/buttery spread
½ cup applesauce
⅓ cup peanut butter or nut butter
    made from cashews or almonds
2 tablespoons molasses
1 teaspoon vanilla extract
⅔ cup gluten-free rolled oats*
¾ cup gluten-free chocolate chips or
    raisins

1. Preheat oven to 325°F. Lightly grease cookie sheet or line with parchment paper.

2. In food processor, combine egg, butter, applesauce, molasses, and vanilla until well blended. Add dry ingredients and rolled oats to food processor. Pulse until thoroughly mixed. Gently stir in chocolate chips (or raisins). Dough will be somewhat stiff.

3. Drop by tablespoons (or use spring-action ice cream scoop for evenly shaped cookies) onto prepared cookie sheet. Flatten each cookie to ½-inch thickness with wet spatula.

4. Bake 20 to 25 minutes or until edges begin to brown. Cool on baking sheet 5 minutes. Transfer cookies to wire rack to cool completely. Makes 12.
Calories 250; Fat 11g; Protein 4g; Carbohydrates 36g; Sodium 215mg; Cholesterol 30mg; Fiber 2g

*Available from www.bobsredmill.com, www.creamhillestates.com, www.giftsofnature.net, www.glutenfreeoats.com, or www.onlyoats.com. Check with your physician to see if these oats are right for you.

∾• Peanut Butter Cookies •∾

These cookies evoke memories of childhood and happy times.

¾ cup creamy peanut butter	1 ¼ cups Flour Blend (page 41)
1 cup packed light brown sugar	½ teaspoon xanthan gum
1 teaspoon vanilla extract	½ teaspoon salt
1 large egg	½ teaspoon baking soda

1. Preheat oven to 375°F. Combine peanut butter, sugar, vanilla, and egg. Beat until well blended.

2. Combine dry ingredients and add to creamed mixture at low speed. Mix just until blended. Flatten dough into disc and refrigerate, covered, for one hour.

3. Shape into 20 balls and place 2 inches apart on large ungreased or parchment-lined cookie sheet. Flatten slightly with tines of fork in crisscross pattern. Freeze 30 minutes.

4. Bake 7 to 8 minutes or until edges start to set and begin to brown. Cool 5 minutes; then transfer to wire rack to cool completely. Makes 20.
Calories 130; Fat 5g; Protein 3g; Carbohydrates 19g; Sodium 144mg; Cholesterol 11mg; Fiber 1g

ଔ• Chocolate Brownies •ଊ

These are wickedly decadent—fudgy and chewy.

1 cup Flour Blend (page 41)
½ cup unsweetened natural cocoa
  (not Dutch)
½ teaspoon baking powder
½ teaspoon salt
1 teaspoon xanthan gum
¼ cup butter/canola oil

½ cup granulated sugar
½ cup packed light brown sugar
1 large egg
2 teaspoons vanilla extract
⅓ cup warm (110°F) water

1. Preheat oven to 350°F. Generously grease 8-inch square nonstick pan. In a small bowl, whisk together flour, cocoa, baking powder, salt, and xanthan gum.
.

2. In large mixing bowl, beat the butter (room temperature) and sugars with electric mixer on medium speed until well combined. Add egg and vanilla; beat until well combined.

3. With mixer on low speed, add dry ingredients and warm water. Mix until just blended. Gently stir in chocolate chips and nuts (see below).

4. Spread batter in prepared pan and bake 20 minutes or until toothpick inserted in center comes out not quite clean. Don't overbake or the brownies won't be fudgy. Cool brownies before cutting. Serves 12.

Calories 155g; Fat 5g; Protein 2g; Carbohydrates 28g; Sodium 117mg; Cholesterol 28mg; Fiber 1g

☙ Double Chocolate Nut Brownies ❧
This Double Chocolate Nut version is incredibly decadent.

1 cup Flour Blend (page 41)
½ cup unsweetened natural cocoa (not Dutch)
½ teaspoon baking powder
½ teaspoon salt
1 teaspoon xanthan gum
¼ cup butter/buttery spread

½ cup granulated sugar
½ cup packed light brown sugar
1 large egg
2 teaspoons vanilla extract
⅓ cup warm (110°F) water
½ cup gluten-free chocolate chips
½ cup chopped walnuts

1. Preheat oven to 350°F. Generously grease 8-inch square nonstick pan. Stir together flour, cocoa, baking powder, salt, and xanthan gum.

2. In large mixing bowl, beat the butter (room temperature) and sugars with electric mixer on medium speed until well combined. Add egg and vanilla; beat until well combined.

3. With mixer on low speed, add dry ingredients and warm water. Mix until just blended. Gently stir in chocolate chips and nuts.

4. Spread batter in prepared pan and bake 20 minutes or until toothpick inserted in center comes out clean. Cool brownies before cutting. Serves 12.
Calories 220; Fat 10g; Protein 3g,; Carbohydrates 33g; Sodium 122mg; Cholesterol 30mg; Fiber 2g

↺• Lemon Bars •↻

The new non-hydrogenated shortenings from Spectrum® or Smart Balance® will work in this family favorite. The tart lemon flavor will have you yearning for more.

Crust
1 cup Flour Blend (page 41)
¼ cup shortening, cold butter or
 buttery spread (not diet)
1 teaspoon xanthan gum
¼ cup powdered sugar
⅛ teaspoon salt

Filling
1 cup powdered sugar
½ cup Flour Blend (page 41)
1 whole egg plus yolks to equal ½ cup
2 tablespoons lemon juice
1 tablespoon grated lemon peel
½ teaspoon xanthan gum
⅛ teaspoon salt
Extra powdered sugar for dusting

1. Preheat oven to 350°F. Grease 8-inch square nonstick pan.

Crust
In food processor, blend the crust ingredients together until crumbly. Press on bottom of pan, using plastic wrap to prevent sticking to hands. Bake 10 to 15 minutes or until browned. Cool slightly.

Filling
In same food processor, combine first seven ingredients and blend until mixture thickens. Pour over crust. Bake 20 to 25 minutes or until browned. Cool completely. Dust with powdered sugar. Cut into 12 pieces. Serves 12.

Calories 180g; Fat 8g; Protein 2g; Carbohydrates 26g; Sodium 54mg; Cholesterol 130mg; Fiber <1g

❧ Seven-Layer Bars ❧

How can we forget this decadent dessert from our childhood! Instead of the usual graham cracker crumbs, use crushed rice bran crackers from Health Valley or your favorite crushed gluten-free cookies such as Pamela's or Enjoy Life Foods.

½ cup butter/buttery spread, melted
2 cups gluten-free cracker or cookie
  crumbs
1 can (14.5 ounces) sweetened condensed
  milk or ⅔ cup whole milk (cow, rice,
  soy)

1 cup gluten-free chocolate chips
1 cup gluten-free butterscotch chips
1 package (7 ounces) sweetened
  shredded coconut
1 cup chopped walnuts

1. Preheat oven to 350°F. Stir together melted butter and cracker crumbs. Press into bottom of greased 13 x 9-inch nonstick pan.

2. Pour sweetened condensed milk over crumbs. Sprinkle with chocolate chips, butterscotch morsels, coconut, and nuts. Gently press mixture down to uniform thickness with spatula.

3. Bake 25 to 30 minutes or until coconut is lightly browned. Cool 45 minutes on wire rack before cutting. Cut into 24 bars. Serves 24 (1 bar each).

Calories 275; Fat 16g; Protein 3g; Carbohydrates 29g; Sodium 102mg; Cholesterol 18mg; Fiber 1g

⟋• Crispy Rice Bars •⟋

These bars are the traditional comfort food for children (and those of us who still like them). Gluten-free marshmallow brands include Kraft Jet-Puffed, International Home Foods, and Campfire. Gluten-free puffed rice cereal brands include Erewhon's Crispy Brown Rice.

⅓ cup butter or margarine
⅓ cup natural peanut butter
1 teaspoon vanilla extract
⅛ teaspoon salt

1 package (5 ½ cups) miniature marsh mallows or 55 large marshmallows
6 cups gluten-free puffed rice cereal
1 cup gluten-free chocolate chips

1. In large saucepan over low heat, melt butter, peanut butter, vanilla, and salt. Add marshmallows and stir until melted and mixture is smooth. Remove from heat.

2. Immediately add cereal and stir with spatula until thoroughly mixed together.

3. Press into greased 13 x 9-inch pan. Immediately, top with chocolate chips and spread them across the top as they melt. Cool completely. Cut into 24 squares. Serves 24 (1 square each).

Calories 150; Fat 6g; Protein 2g; Carbohydrates 21g; Sodium 45mg; Cholesterol 8mg; Fiber <1g

☞• Pie Crust (Double-Crust) •☜

Gluten-free pie crusts are not impossible! This one rolls out beautifully. With a little practice, you'll be a pro. This crust works best with stone fruit fillings like cherries, peaches, or apricots. If you only need a single crust, freeze the remaining half for future use.

1 cup Flour Blend (page 41)	½ teaspoon salt
¾ cup tapioca flour	½ cup shortening,* at room temperature
½ cup sweet rice flour	2 tablespoons butter/buttery spread (non-diet)
1 tablespoon sugar	¼ cup milk (cow, rice, soy)
1 teaspoon xanthan gum	1 whole egg for egg wash (optional)
1 teaspoon guar gum	*Non-hydrogenated shortenings, made by Spectrum® or Smart Balance®, are available at health food stores.*

1. Place dry ingredients, shortening, and butter in food processor. Mix well. Add milk and blend until dough forms ball.

2. Flatten dough to 1-inch disk, wrap tightly, and chill 1 hour so liquids are well distributed throughout dough.

3. Massage dough between hands until warm and pliable, making crust easier to handle. Roll half of dough to 10-inch circle between two pieces of heavy-duty plastic wrap dusted with rice flour. (Use damp paper towel between countertop and plastic wrap to anchor plastic. wrap) (Keep remaining half wrapped tightly to avoid drying out.) Be sure to move rolling pin from center of dough to outer edge, moving around the circle in clockwise fashion to assure uniform thickness.

4. Remove top plastic wrap and invert crust, centering it over a 9-inch nonstick pie plate. Remove remaining plastic wrap and press into place. If dough is hard to handle, press the entire bottom crust in place with your fingers.

5. Fill with your favorite fruit filling for 9-inch pie, but limit the amount of extra juice to 2 tablespoons. See fillings on next page.

6. Roll remaining dough to 10-inch circle between floured plastic wrap. Invert and center on filled crust. Don't remove top plastic wrap until dough is centered. Shape decorative ridge around rim of pie plate. Prick crust several times with fork to allow steam to escape. Freeze 15 minutes. Brush with beaten egg, if desired, for prettier crust. Sprinkle with sugar. Place on nonstick baking sheet.

7. Bake pie in preheated 375°F oven 15 minutes on lower oven rack to brown bottom crust. Move to next highest oven rack and bake another 25 to 35 minutes––or until crust is nicely browned. Cover loosely with foil if edges brown too much. Cool completely on wire rack before cutting. Serves 6.
Crust only:

Calories 375; Fat 22g; Protein 2g; Carbohydrates 44mg; Sodium 203mg; Cholesterol 11mg; Fiber <1g

Cherry Pie*:* Combine 2 cans (about 14.5 ounces each) drained tart red cherries, 2 tablespoons of the cherry juice, ⅔ cup sugar, 1 tablespoon quick-cooking tapioca, and 1 teaspoon almond extract in bowl. Let stand while preparing pie crust. Place in prepared crust. Go to Step 6 above.
Calories 535; Fat 22g; Protein 4g; Carbohydrates 84g; Sodium 208mg; Cholesterol 11mg; Fiber 3g

Peach Pie*:* In large bowl, combine 3 cups (about 3 large) sliced fresh peaches, ½ cup sugar, 2 tablespoons potato starch, 1 teaspoon almond extract, and ¼ teaspoon salt. Just before placing peaches in prepared pie crust, drain all but 2 tablespoons juice. Place peaches in prepared pie crust. Go to Step 6 above.
Calories 482; Fat 22g; Protein 3g; Carbohydrates 72g; Sodium 300mg; Cholesterol 11mg; Fiber 2g

Pumpkin Pie*:* Combine 2 cans (15 ounces each) pumpkin, 1 ½ cup sugar, 4 teaspoons pumpkin pie spice, 2 teaspoons cinnamon, 1 ½ teaspoons salt, 4 eggs, and 2 cups milk or dairy substitute. Pour into two prepared deep-dish pastry shells (bottom crust only) that have been chilled 15 minutes. Bake 15 minutes in preheated 425°F oven on lower rack. Move pies to center rack; reduce heat to 350°F and bake 40 to 50 minutes or until knife inserted near the center comes out clean. Cover edges of crust with foil if they start to brown too much. Cool 2 hours on wire rack. Serve immediately or refrigerate. Makes two pies. Serves 12 (6 slices per pie).
Calories 345; Fat 13g; Protein 5g; Carbohydrates 54g; Sodium 435mg;Cholesterol 80mg; Fiber 1g

☞• Flourless Pie Crusts for No-Bake Pies •☜

For those times when you don't want or need a flaky, pastry-type crust, the following crust provide wonderful variety, texture, and taste.

Chocolate Peanut Butter Crust: Melt ¾ cup gluten-free chocolate chips and 2 tablespoons peanut butter (or butter/buttery spread) over low heat. Remove from heat and stir in 1 cup Barbara's® Brown Rice Crisps. Spread crust in greased 9 or 10-inch pie plate. Chill until firm. Add filling. Bring to room temperature before serving for easier cutting. Serves 6.
Calories 160; Fat 9g; Protein 3g; Carbohydrates 19g; Sodium 43mg; Cholesterol 5mg; Fiber 1g

Coconut Pie Crust: Grease 9-inch pie plate. Combine 1 ½ cups shredded coconut, 2 tablespoons soft butter or margarine, 1 tablespoon sweet rice flour, 1 teaspoon vanilla extract, and ¼ teaspoon salt. Press onto bottom and up sides of 9-inch pie plate. Bake at 325°F until lightly toasted—about 10 to 15 minutes. Watch carefully to avoid burning. Cool thoroughly. Add filling of your choice. Serves 6.
Calories 160; Fat 12g; Protein <1g; Carbohydrates 13g; Sodium 148mg; Cholesterol 10mg; Fiber 1g

Crumb Pie Crust: In food processor, thoroughly combine 1 cup crushed cookie crumbs (e.g., Pamela's® cookies or Health Valley® Rice Bran crackers or Nutty Rice Cereal from Enjoy Life Foods®), ¼ cup butter or margarine (room temperature), ¼ cup finely ground nuts, and 2 tablespoons sugar. Press into greased 9-inch microwave-safe pie plate. Microwave 2 to 3 minutes on high until firm. Add filling and chill until ready to serve. Serves 6.
Calories 165; Fat 12g; Protein 1g; Carbohydrates 14g; Sodium 43mg; Cholesterol 0mg; Fiber <1g

ℭ⋅ Peach or Cherry Cobbler ⋅℥

Substitute your own favorite fruit—perhaps cherries or blueberries—in this family favorite. Be sure to shake the buttermilk thoroughly before measuring.

1 cup Flour Blend (page 41)
½ cup sugar
1 teaspoon baking powder
½ teaspoon xanthan gum
¼ teaspoon salt
¼ cup cold butter/buttery spread
1 large egg

1 teaspoon grated lemon peel
1 teaspoon vanilla extract
⅓ cup buttermilk or ½ teaspoon vinegar
   plus enough milk (cow, rice, soy) to
   equal ⅓ cup
1 teaspoon sugar (to sprinkle on topping)

Peach Cobbler Filling

Grease 11 x 7-inch pan. In large bowl, combine 3 cups (about 3 large) sliced fresh peaches and 1 tablespoon sugar. Let stand 30 minutes. Drain. Combine ½ cup sugar, 2 tablespoons potato starch, and ¼ teaspoon each cinnamon, nutmeg, and salt. Toss with drained peaches and 1 teaspoon almond extract. Place in prepared pan. Add cobbler topping. Bake as directed above. Serves 6.

Calories 345; Fat 9g; Protein 3g; Carbohydrates 66g; Sodium 162mg; Cholesterol 56mg; Fiber 2g

Cherry Cobbler Filling

Grease 8 x 8-inch pan. Combine 2 cans (about 14.5 ounces each) drained tart red cherries, ¼ cup of the cherry juice, ⅔ cup sugar, 1 tablespoon quick-cooking tapioca, and 1 teaspoon almond extract in pan. Let stand while preparing cobbler topping. Add cobbler topping and bake as directed. Serves 6.

Calories 395; Fat 9g; Protein 4g; Carbohydrates 77g; Sodium 167mg; Cholesterol 56mg; Fiber 3g

Topping

Preheat oven to 375°F. Combine dry ingredients; cut in butter. Whisk together buttermilk, egg, lemon peel, and vanilla. Stir into dry ingredients until just mixed. Drop by tablespoonfuls on filling, which will spread out as it bakes. Sprinkle with sugar. Bake on middle oven rack 35 to 40 minutes or until nicely browned.

 Carol's Tip: No buttermilk? Add 1 Tablespoon vinegar or lemon juice to 1 cup milk (this works with cow, soy or nut milk, but not as well with rice milk). Let stand for a few minutes to thicken.

❧• Apple Crisp •❧

You can substitute pears or peaches in this easy home-style dessert.

Filling

3 cups sliced apples (Gala, Granny Smith, or your choice)

2 tablespoons juice (apple, orange)

2 tablespoons maple syrup

½ teaspoon cornstarch

1 teaspoon vanilla extract

¼ teaspoon ground cinnamon

¼ teaspoon salt

Topping

¼ cup gluten-free rolled oats*

¼ cup Flour Blend (page 41)

¼ cup finely chopped nuts

2 tablespoons maple syrup

2 tablespoons soft butter/buttery spread

1 teaspoon vanilla extract

¼ teaspoon ground cinnamon

¼ teaspoon salt

1. Preheat oven to 375°F. Toss all filling ingredients in 8 x 8-inch greased pan.

2. In small bowl, combine topping ingredients. Sprinkle over apple mixture. Cover with foil; bake 25 minutes. Uncover; bake another 15 minutes or until topping is crisp. (Top with vanilla ice cream or whipped cream.) Serves 6.
Calories 175; Fat 6g; Protein 1g; Carbohydrates 28g; Sodium 197mg; Cholesterol 10mg; Fiber 3g

*Available from www.bobsredmill.com, www.creamhillestates.com, www.giftsofnature.net, www.glutenfreeoats.com, or www.onlyoats.com. Check with your physician to see if these oats are right for you.

◌◦ Chocolate Pudding ◦◌

This is comfort food at its best! Use 4 tbsp cornstarch if using rice milk.

½ cup white or brown sugar
⅓ cup unsweetened cocoa
3 tablespoons cornstarch
⅛ teaspoon salt

2 cups milk (cow, rice, soy)
1 tablespoon butter/buttery spread
1 teaspoon vanilla extract

Whisk together first four ingredients in saucepan. Gradually whisk in milk. Bring to boil over medium heat, whisking constantly; cook for one minute—continuing to whisk. Remove from heat; add butter and vanilla. Pour into four goblets or bowls. Chill two hours. Makes 2 cups. Serves 4 (½ cup each).

Calories 230; Fat 6g; Protein 6g; Carbohydrates 42g; Sodium 147mg; Cholesterol 17mg; Fiber 2g

◌◦ Vanilla Pudding ◦◌

Use this versatile custard in pies, cake fillings...or just by itself!

1 ½ cups milk (cow, rice, soy)
½ cup sugar
2 tablespoons cornstarch

4 large egg yolks (room temperature)
1 tablespoon butter/buttery spread
2 teaspoons vanilla extract

1. Heat milk to 120°F in heavy saucepan. Set aside.

2. In a small bowl, whisk sugar and cornstarch together. In another small bowl, beat egg yolks with electric mixer until thick and lemon-colored. Slowly add cornstarch mixture, mixing thoroughly until smooth.

3. Gradually whisk egg yolk mixture into hot milk. Cook over low-medium heat 2 to 3 minutes, whisking constantly, until thickened.

4. Remove from heat. Stir in butter and vanilla extract. Transfer to bowl; cover with plastic wrap touching surface of custard to prevent skin formation. Refrigerate until chilled. Stir before serving. Makes about 2 cups. Serves 4 (½ cup each).

Calories 250; Fat 10g; Protein 6g; Carbohydrates 34g; Sodium 54mg; Cholesterol 228mg; Fiber <1g

⋄• Pudding Mix •⋄

Keep this easy mix in your pantry for quick puddings. It makes 5 recipes.

8 cups nonfat dry milk powder (cow, rice, soy-not Carnation))

2 cups sugar

1 cup cornstarch

1 teaspoon salt

Chocolate Pudding

Whisk together 2 cups water, 2 cups Pudding Mix, and ¼ cup Dutch cocoa in heavy saucepan over medium-high heat. Continue whisking until mixture boils. Remove from heat. Stir in 1 teaspoon vanilla. Cool. Makes 4 servings (½ cup each).

Calories.230; Fat 6g; Protein 6g; Carbohydrates 42g; Sodium 147mg;Cholesterol 17mg; Fiber 2g

Vanilla Pudding

In heavy saucepan, whisk together 2 cups water and 4 egg yolks until very smooth. Whisk in 2 cups Pudding Mix. Place pan over medium-high heat and continue whisking until mixture thickens. Remove from heat, stir in 1 teaspoon vanilla. Cool. Makes 4 servings (½ cup each).

Calories 250; Fat 10g; Protein 6g;Carbohydrates 34g; Sodium 54mg; Cholesterol 228mg; Fiber <1g

 Carol's Tip: Non-dairy milk powders such as Solait, Better Than Milk, or DariFree can be used in place of dry milk powder. Make sure the rice version of Better Than Milk is the newer, gluten-free formula.

❧ Main Dishes & Miscellaneous ❧

Casseroles, One-Dish Meals, and Old Favorites

For more delicious main dishes:

Wheat-Free Recipes & Menus: Delicious, Healthful Eating for People with Food Sensitivities by Carol Fenster, Ph.D.
Cooking Free: 200 Flavorful Recipes for People with Food Allergies & Multiple Food Sensitivities by Carol Fenster, Ph.D.
Gluten-Free Quick & Easy--From Prep to Plate without the Fuss by Carol Fenster, Ph.D.
1,000 Gluten-Free Recipes by Carol Fenster, Ph.D.

❧ Chicken Fingers ☙

These are very similar to those on the menu at fast food restaurants.

4 boneless, skinless chicken breast halves (very cold)
1 egg, beaten (very cold)

½ cup very cold milk (cow, rice, soy
1 cup Basic Breading mix (page 41)
¼ cup canola or peanut oil (for frying)

1. Slice each chicken breast diagonally into ½-inch wide strips. Whisk together egg and milk.

2. Dip each strip into egg mixture, then into breading mix. Fry in oil until browned. Add salt and pepper to taste. Or, bake on non-stick baking sheet 30 minutes at 350°F or until browned. Serves 4.

Calories 375; Fat 19g; Protein 32g; Carbohydrates 17g; Cholesterol 136 mg; Sodium 118mg; Fiber <1g

❧ Fish Sticks ☙

Kids love fish sticks and it's a great way to use up left over cooked fish.

1 pound cooked fish
  (cod, perch, sole, snapper)
2 large eggs, divided
1 tablespoon Dijon mustard
½ teaspoon dried thyme

¼ teaspoon salt
¼ teaspoon pepper
1 cup gluten-free bread crumbs, divided
2 tablespoons chopped chives or onions
2 tablespoons canola or peanut oil (for frying)

1. Place half of fish in food processor, *one* of the eggs, mustard, thyme, salt, pepper, and ¼ cup bread crumbs. Puree until smooth.

2. Flake remaining fish with fork. Stir in pureed fish, chives, or onions. Shape into 4 patties or 8 sticks.

3. In separate bowl, whisk remaining egg until foamy. Place remaining bread crumbs on plate. Dip fish patties first into egg, then into crumbs.

4. Fry fish in oil over medium-high heat until golden brown on one side. Turn; fry until cooked through (about 2 to 3 minutes each side). Serves 4 (1 patty each or 2 sticks each).

Calories: 350; Fat 16g,;Protein 30g; Carbohydrates 21g; Sodium 570mg; Cholesterol 173mg; Fiber <1g

Chicken-Fried Steak & Gravy

This is the comfort food many of us associate with home cooking.

4 cube steaks (4 to 6 ounces each)
⅓ cup Flour Blend (page 41)
½ teaspoon salt
½ teaspoon black pepper
½ teaspoon paprika
¼ teaspoon onion powder

2 tablespoons canola oil
1 cup milk (cow, rice, soy—divided)
2 teaspoons cornstarch or potato starch
¼ teaspoon salt
¼ teaspoon black pepper

1. Pat steaks dry and set aside.

2. Combine flour blend, salt, pepper, paprika, and onion powder on plate. Dredge steaks in flour mixture; pound with spatula to make flour adhere to meat.

3. Heat cooking oil in non-stick skillet. Brown steaks on both sides; then cook to desired doneness. Remove from skillet and cover to keep warm.

4. Mix cornstarch with ¼ cup of the milk. Stir into pan over low-medium heat, scraping up browned bits in skillet. Add remaining milk and cook, stirring constantly, until mixture thickens. Add salt and pepper. Pour into gravy server and keep warm.

5. Return steaks to skillet to gently reheat. Serve warm with gravy on the side. Makes 4 servings (1 steak each).

Calories 390; Fat 28g; Protein 18g; Carbohydrates 15g; Sodium 520mg;Cholesterol 69mg; Fiber <1g

ℭ𝔰• Oven-Fried Chicken •𝔰𝔬

This is a low-calorie version, baked in an oven, but it still tastes wonderful. Gluten-free brands of cornmeal include Albers, Lamb's, Kinnikinnick, and Shiloh Farms.

½ cup buttermilk or ½ teaspoon
   vinegar plus enough milk (cow, rice, soy)
     to equal ½ cup
¼ teaspoon cayenne pepper
¼ teaspoon garlic powder
¼ cup brown rice flour

3 tablespoons gluten-free cornmeal
½ teaspoon salt
¼ teaspoon white pepper
¼ teaspoon paprika
4 skinless chicken thighs

1. Preheat oven to 400°F. Grease baking sheet.

2. In bowl, mix buttermilk, cayenne pepper, and garlic powder.

3. In shallow bowl, mix dry ingredients together. Dip each chicken thigh into buttermilk mixture; then into flour mixture. Place on prepared baking pan. Gently mist chicken pieces with cooking spray.

4. Bake 45 to 60 minutes or until chicken is crispy and done. Serves 4.
Calories 200; Fat 2g; Protein 29g; Carbohydrates 14g; Sodium 400mg; Cholesterol 70mg; Fiber 1g

Additional Breading Ideas

Fried chicken (or any fried meat or vegetable) can be breaded with any of the following. Dip in milk, buttermilk, or beaten egg first. Each breading produces a different texture and taste.

Amaranth flakes (NuWorld Amaranth, NuWorld Foods)
Cornflakes (Nature's Path)
Cornmeal
Cream of Rice cereal
Crushed corn tortilla chips

Crushed rice crackers
Gluten-free bread crumbs
Mashed potato flakes
Southern Homestyle cornflake crumbs
Southern Homestyle tortilla crumbs

ଓଃ• Gravy •ଚ୍ଚ

This is a basic recipe using turkey or chicken drippings, which are what remains in the roasting pan after the meat is roasted. You can vary the flavor with your favorite herbs ands spices.

1 ¾ cups chicken broth, divided
½ cup strained drippings
Thickener of your choice:
   Cornstarch: 2 tablespoons
   Rice flour: 4 tablespoons
   Sweet rice flour: 4 tablespoons
   Tapioca flour: 6 tablespoons

¼ teaspoon salt
¼ teaspoon black pepper
¼ teaspoon ground sage
¼ teaspoon dried thyme leaves
¼ teaspoon poultry seasoning

1. Combine strained drippings and broth in heavy saucepan, reserving ½ cup of the broth. (To lower the fat content, skim the fat off the top or freeze it for 15 minutes so fat congeals and can be removed—or use a specially designed measuring cup that allows you to pour the drippings from the bottom, leaving the fat in the cup.

2. Place pan over medium-high heat, adding seasonings. Stir thickener into ½ cup reserved broth, making a thin paste. Gently whisk thickening mixture into pan, continuing to whisk until mixture thickens and boils. Adjust consistency by adding more thickener or chicken broth. Remove from heat. Strain, if desired. Taste and adjust seasonings, if necessary. Makes 2 ¼ cups. Serves 8 (about ¼ cup gravy each).

Calories 140; Fat 14g; Protein 1g; Carbohydrates 2g; Sodium 186mg; Cholesterol 14mg; Fiber <1g
Nutrient content calculated without fat-lowering techniques

Note: Each thickener products a different type of gravy. Cornstarch produces a smoother, low gloss gravy. Rice flour, given its grittiness, produces a somewhat grainy gravy with a dull, opaque look. Sweet rice flour produces a smoother, whiter-colored gravy with a nice mouth-feel. Tapioca flour gives the gravy a low gloss sheen, but also a somewhat unusual texture. At my house we use cornstarch or sweet rice flour.

∞• Ham & Scalloped Potatoes •∞

This has long been one of our family's favorite dishes. It's actually quite easy to make and is good as leftovers.

4 medium russet potatoes (peeled, sliced)
1 cup cubed ham
1 tablespoon instant minced onion
½ teaspoon onion salt
¼ teaspoon white pepper
½ teaspoon dry mustard*
⅛ teaspoon ground nutmeg

2 tablespoons potato starch or sweet rice flour
2 cups milk (cow, rice, soy)
1 tablespoon canola oil
1 tablespoon Parmesan cheese (cow, rice, soy)
1 tablespoon butter/buttery spread, cubed
Paprika for garnish
*Grind your own mustard seeds with small coffee grinder or use Durkee or McCormick.

1. Preheat oven to 350°F. Toss potatoes and ham with onion, salt, and pepper in 1 ½-quart casserole or baking dish. In jar with screw top lid, shake together mustard, nutmeg, and potato starch. Add milk, oil, and Parmesan cheese, and shake thoroughly until ingredients are blended. Or, blend in blender until smooth.

2. Pour milk mixture over potatoes and ham. Dot with butter cubes. Lightly sprinkle with paprika. Bake 1 hour or until sauce is bubbly and potatoes are lightly browned. Serves 4.
Calories:380; Fat 13g; Protein 19g; Carbohydrates 49g; Sodium 345mg; Cholesterol 50mg; Fiber 4g

☞ Spicy Breaded Chicken ☜

Here's another way to prepare crispy oven-fried chicken. Gluten-free brands of cornmeal include Albers, Lamb's, Kinnikinnick, and Shiloh Farms.

1 cup very finely crushed corn chips
1 teaspoon salt
½ teaspoon garlic powder
½ teaspoon ground cumin
½ teaspoon black pepper
¼ teaspoon cayenne pepper
4 chicken breast halves
   (boneless and skinless)

Preheat oven to 400ºF. Combine dry ingredients. Roll chicken in mixture; place on greased baking sheet. Bake 20 minutes; turn and bake 15 to 20 minutes or until done. Serves 4.

Calories: 170; Fat 4g; Protein 28g; Carbohydrates 4g; Sodium 699mg; Cholesterol 68mg; Fiber <1g

☞ Basic Breading Mix ☜

Keep this mix on hand for a last-minute meal. It works great on meat and vegetables. Gluten-free brands of cornmeal include Albers, Lamb's, Kinnikinnick, and Shiloh Farms.

1 cup yellow or white gluten-free
   cornmeal
1 cup cornstarch
1 teaspoon dried thyme
1 teaspoon dried oregano
1 teaspoon onion powder
1 teaspoon paprika
1 teaspoon salt
½ teaspoon cayenne pepper
¼ teaspoon garlic powder
¼ teaspoon sugar

Mix ingredients together and store in airtight container in dark, dry place. Use as breading mix for meats, seafood, or vegetables in frying and baking. Do not reuse mix after dipping. Use within 3 months. Makes 2 cups or 32 tablespoons.

Per tablespoon:
Calories 35; Fat 0g; Protein 1g; Carbohydrates 8g; Sodium 80mg; Cholesterol 0mg; Fiber 1g

❧ French Fried Onions ❧

If you're craving French fried onions, you'll love this recipe. You can add your own favorite seasoning to the batter or sprinkle it on later.

2 large onions in ¼-inch slices　　**¼ teaspoon garlic powder**
1 recipe Breading Batter (below)　　**Peanut oil for frying**
¼ teaspoon salt

1. Combine Basic Breading Batter with salt and garlic powder. Dip sliced onions into mixture, coating thoroughly.

2. Heat 2 inches of oil to 375°F in Dutch oven. Add ¼ of the onions to hot oil and fry until golden brown on both sides, turning once. Drain on paper towels. Fry remaining onions in same manner (about ¼ at a time), adding more oil if necessary to keep onions constantly immersed.

Calories 250; Fat 15g; Protein 4g; Carbohydrates 25g; Sodium 207mg; Cholesterol 5mg; Fiber 2g

❧ Basic Breading Batter ❧

This batter makes a nice, crispy coating on fried foods. Peanut oil is the best option; however, other oils work well, too. Gluten-free brands of cornmeal include Albers, Lamb's, Kinnikinnick, and Shiloh Farms.

¼ cup Flour Blend (page 41)　　**¼ teaspoon salt**
¼ cup cornmeal　　**¼ teaspoon white pepper**
2 teaspoons sugar　　**1 cup milk (cow, rice, soy)**
½ teaspoon baking powder　　**Peanut oil for frying**

Whisk all ingredients together. Dip meat (fish fillets, shrimp, flattened chicken breasts, or ground chicken balls) and fry on medium heat in peanut oil until golden brown. Makes about 1 cup batter. Discard unused batter.

Calories 220; Fat 15g; Protein 3g; Carbohydrates 18g; Sodium 205mg; Cholesterol 5mg; Fiber <1g

 Carol's Tip: Chill batter one hour for an even crispier crust. It should be no thicker than heavy cream for best results.

☞ Macaroni & Cheese ☜

I know it's faster to just open a package of macaroni and cheese, but this homemade version is truly flavorful. Use sharp cheddar for fuller flavor. Beau Monde seasoning is made by Spice Islands.

2 cups grated cheddar cheese (cow, rice, soy)
½ pound gluten-free pasta, cooked al dente*
2 tablespoons cornstarch
½ teaspoon dry mustard**
¼ teaspoon white pepper

*I recommend elbow macaroni pasta by Pastariso, DeBole, Tinkyada, or Heartland's Finest. Or, Dr. Schar penne pasta www.glutensolutions.com , www.glutenfreepantry.com

⅛ teaspoon cayenne pepper
½ teaspoon Beau Monde seasoning
1 ¾ cups milk (cow, rice, soy)
1 teaspoon Worcestershire sauce (Lea & Perrin's is gluten-free in the U.S.)
Garnish with dash of paprika

**Grind your own mustard seeds with a small coffee grinder or use Durkee or McCormick.

1. Have grated cheddar cheese ready and pasta cooked al dente (slightly underdone—it continues to cook for awhile).

2. Combine cornstarch, mustard, peppers, and Beau Monde seasoning. Then stir into milk combined with Worcestershire sauce. Place over medium heat in large saucepan and whisk until mixture thickens. Stir in cheese until melted.

3. Toss with cooked pasta and serve immediately with a garnish of fresh parsley and a dash of paprika. Serves 4.

Calories: 335; Fat 8g; Protein 24g; Carbohydrates 42g; Sodium 445mg;, Cholesterol 62mg; Fiber 2g

ᏨᎦ• Meat Loaf •ᏑᎤ

My gluten-eating friends prefer this flavorful, gluten-free version instead of their own!

1 can (8 ounces) tomato sauce
¼ cup packed light brown sugar
½ teaspoon dry mustard*
½ teaspoon chili powder
¼ teaspoon ground cloves
1 garlic clove, minced
1 teaspoon Worcestershire sauce
   (Lea & Perrin's is gluten-free in
   the U.S.)

* *Grind your own mustard seeds with a small coffee grinder or use Durkee or McCormick.*

1 pound lean ground beef
1 large egg, beaten
1 cup gluten-free bread crumbs**
½ teaspoon salt
¼ teaspoon black pepper
1 tablespoon instant minced onion

**Or use 1 cup of the following: crushed rice crackers, corn flakes (Erewhon), mashed potato flakes, rolled rice or quinoa flakes, cream of rice cereal flakes, or cream of buckwheat cereal flakes.*

1. Preheat oven to 350ºF. In small bowl, combine tomato sauce sugar, mustard, chili powder, cloves, garlic, and Worcestershire sauce. Mix well.

2. In large bowl, put one half of tomato mixture. Add ground beef, egg, breadcrumbs, salt, pepper, and onion. Mix well with hands.

3. Shape into loaf, either rounded or rectangular; place in baking pan. If desired, place loaf on metal rack in pan. (I use a round, perforated rack which allows fat to drip through to the bottom of the pan, yet Meat Loaf does not sit in this fat during baking). Make indentation in center of loaf and pour remaining tomato mixture into this indentation.

4. Bake 45 minutes, or until nicely browned. Serves 4.
Calories 395; Fat 13g; Protein 29g; Carbohydrates 39g; Sodium 990mg; Cholesterol 94mg,;Fiber 2g

೧•ﾟ Pizza •ﾟ੭

This pizza crust is so delicious that it has received national acclaim. You can hold it in your hand and it won't crumble!

Crust
1 tablespoon active dry yeast
¾ cup warm (110°F) milk(cow, rice, soy)
½ teaspoon sugar
⅔ cup garbanzo/fava bean flour or brown rice flour
½ cup tapioca flour
2 teaspoons xanthan gum
½ teaspoon salt
1 teaspoon unflavored gelatin powder
1 teaspoon Italian seasoning
1 teaspoon olive oil
1 teaspoon cider vinegar

Sauce
1 can (8 ounces) tomato sauce
½ teaspoon dried oregano
½ teaspoon dried basil
½ teaspoon dried rosemary
½ teaspoon fennel seeds
¼ teaspoon garlic powder
 or 1 minced garlic clove
2 teaspoons sugar
½ teaspoon salt

Sauce
Combine ingredients in small saucepan. Simmer 15 minutes. Makes about 1 cup or enough for 12-inch pizza. Serves 6.

Crust
1. Preheat oven to 425°F. Dissolve yeast and sugar in warm milk for five minutes. In food processor, blend all crust ingredients, including yeast mixture, until ball forms. Dough will be soft.

2. Put mixture into greased 12-inch nonstick pizza pan. Liberally sprinkle rice flour onto dough; then press dough into pan with hands, continuing to dust dough with flour to prevent sticking. Make edges thicker to contain toppings.

3. Bake pizza crust 10 minutes. Remove from oven. Add sauce and toppings to crust. Bake another 20 to 25 minutes or until top is nicely browned. Serves 6. (1 slice each).
Calories 105; Fat 2g; Protein 4g; Carbohydrates 19g; Sodium 652mg; Cholesterol 2mg; Fiber 2g

 Carol's Tip: See Pizza 101—a step-by-step guide to making gluten-free pizza at www.glutenfree101.com. Click on Recipes, then on Pizza, then on Pizza 101

ೞ• Easy Quiche •ಖ

You won't believe how this recipe miraculously turns into a quiche that is perfect for dinner, lunch, or brunch. Pair it with crusty bread and a salad. Beau Monde seasoning is made by Spice Islands.

1 cup finely diced ham
1 cup Swiss or gruyere cheese
  (shredded – cow, rice, soy))
1 ¾ cups milk (cow, rice, soy)
¾ cup Flour Blend (page 41)
¼ cup dried minced onions

¼ cup melted butter/buttery spread
2 tablespoons grated Parmesan cheese
  (cow, rice, soy)
¼ teaspoon Beau Monde seasoning
⅛ teaspoon ground nutmeg

1. Preheat oven to 400°F. Lightly grease 9-inch pie plate. Sprinkle ham and cheese in plate. Whisk together remaining ingredients until smooth. Pour over ham and cheese.

2. Bake 30 to 40 minutes or until top is golden brown. Cool on wire rack for 5 minutes before cutting into 6 slices. Serves 6.

Calories 285; Fat 17g; Protein 14g; Carbohydrates 19g; Sodium 500mg; Cholesterol 57mg; Fiber <1g

❧ Spaghetti & Meatballs ❧

This has been my family heirloom recipe for over 30 years. I promise you'll love it.

Meatballs
1 pound ground round
¼ teaspoon salt
½ teaspoon black pepper
¼ cup gluten-free bread crumbs
1 large egg
2 tablespoons dried parsley
1 ½ teaspoons basil
½ teaspoon dried oregano
1 clove garlic, minced
2 tablespoons Romano cheese
¼ teaspoon crushed red pepper

Sauce
1 can (24 ounces) tomato juice
2 cans (6 ounces each) tomato paste
1 ½ tablespoons dried parsley
1 ½ tablespoons sugar
1 tablespoon dried basil
1 ½ teaspoons dried rosemary
1 bay leaf
1 teaspoon dried oregano
1 teaspoon salt (to taste)
½ teaspoon black pepper
2 tablespoons Romano cheese
  (optional)

2 pounds gluten-free spaghetti, (cooked)
DeBole's, Annie's, Heartland Ingredients, Tinkyada, and Pastariso are good.
Order Dr. Schaer's from www.glutensolutions.com or www.glutenfreepantry.com

Meatballs

1. Preheat oven to 350°F. Combine all ingredients in large bowl and mix well with hands. Shape into 1 ½-inch balls and place on baking sheet. Bake 20 minutes. Remove from oven; cool on sheet 15 minutes. Serve with sauce and spaghetti. Serves 12.

2. Add cooled meatballs to Spaghetti Sauce. Serve over cooked spaghetti. Serves 6.

Sauce

Combine all ingredients in slow cooker. Mix well. Cook all day on low-medium heat. Stir occasionally. Serves 6.

Calories 240; Fat 4g; Protein 13g; Carbohydrates 42g; Sodium 345mg; Cholesterol 40mg.; Fiber 6g

 Carol's Tip: For uniform browning, less fat, and to keep the meat balls round, bake 20 to 25 minutes on foil-lined baking sheet in 350°F oven.

ଓ୪• Penne Pasta Casserole •ଧ୦

This was an old stand-by for busy nights when I was late getting home from work.
I could have a meal on the table in 30 minutes! This easy pasta dish cooks on the stove
while you fix the remaining dishes—salad and perhaps a crusty bread.

½ pound lean ground beef
2 cups uncooked gluten-free penne
pasta*
1 can (15 ounces) diced tomatoes
*DeBole's, Annie's, Heartland's Finest, and
Pastariso are good. Order Dr. Schar pasta at
www.glutensolutions.com,www.glutenfreepantry.com

1 tablespoon dried minced onion
1 teaspoon Worcestershire sauce (Lea
& Perrin's is gluten-free in the U.S.)
1 teaspoon onion powder
1 teaspoon seasoning salt

1. Brown ground beef in large skillet. Add uncooked pasta, along with remaining ingredients.

2. Bring to boil, cover with lid, and reduce heat to low-medium. Cook until pasta is done, stirring occasionally to prevent sticking. Dish is done when liquid has been absorbed by pasta. Serves 4.
Calories 260; Fat 3g; Protein 18g; Carbohydrates 40g; Sodium 427mg; Cholesterol 30mg; Fiber 4g

❧ Six-Layer Casserole ❧

My mother-in-law made this casserole during my husband's childhood. When we married, he asked me to continue making it for him. It is super-easy and can be assembled the night before, then baked the next day. Plan ahead...it takes 2 hours to bake, but it's worth the wait! Leftovers are good, too.

1 large raw potato, thinly sliced
⅓ cup uncooked white rice
½ pound fresh lean ground beef
1 small onion, finely diced
1 cup finely diced carrots
½ cup green peas

4 cups diced canned tomatoes
2 teaspoons salt
1 teaspoon sugar
½ teaspoon thyme
½ teaspoon black pepper

1. Preheat oven to 350°F. Grease deep casserole dish (with 7 to 8 cup capacity).

2. Layer potato over bottom of dish. Top with layer of rice, then ground beef, followed by onion, carrots, and peas.

3. Mix tomatoes with salt, sugar, thyme, and black pepper. Pour into dish. Cover with casserole lid or aluminum foil.

4. Bake 2 hours or until vegetables are done. Remove casserole lid or foil during last 15 minutes of baking for better browning. Serves 6 (1 ½ cups each).
Calories 150; Fat 2g; Protein 11g; Carbohydrates 24g; Sodium 932mg; Cholesterol 20mg; Fiber 4g

ଔ• Pot Pie with Biscuit Topping •ଓ

At my house, if we have roast chicken or roast beef for dinner, it's a sure bet that we'll have pot pie later in the week. If it's roast chicken, we usually use some of the cold chicken for sandwiches and then I use the bones later to make chicken broth. For a healthy variation that adds an interesting texture to the biscuit topping, replace 2 tablespoons of the Flour Blend with Montina pure supplement, available at www.amazinggrains.com.

1 cup Flour Blend (page 41)
½ cup cornstarch or potato starch
1 tablespoon sugar
2 teaspoons baking powder
¼ teaspoon baking soda
1 teaspoon xanthan gum
1 teaspoon guar gum
1 teaspoon herbes de Provence or
    dried thyme leaves

½ teaspoon salt
¼ cup shortening*
¾ cup milk (cow, rice, soy)
1 large egg
Filling to serve 6 people (use beef stew,
    chicken soup, or vegetable stew
    thickened to desired consistency)

*Non-hydrogenated shortening by Spectrum® and Smart Balance® are available at health food stores.

1. Preheat oven to 375ºF. Fill greased 13 x 9-inch casserole dish with filling of choice such as vegetable stew, beef stew, or chicken soup (thickened to desired consistency). Put casserole dish in oven to start baking.

2. Meanwhile, in food processor, pulse dry ingredients (cornstarch through salt) to mix thoroughly. Add shortening, milk, and egg white. Blend until dough forms ball, scraping down sides with spatula, if necessary. Dough will be somewhat soft.

3. Remove casserole from oven and drop biscuit dough by heaping table-spoons onto hot filling. Return to oven and continue baking for another 20 to 25 minutes or until topping is nicely browned. Serve immediately. Serves 6.

Based on using beef stew:
Calories 470; Fat 16g; Protein 26g; Carbohydrates 58g; Sodium 837 mg; Cholesterol 93 mg; Fiber <1g

❧ Pot Pie with Pie Crust Topping ❧

This version of pot pie is a little more refined than the biscuit topping version on the previous page. I use it when I want a topping that is crispy rather than "bready". Don't use "diet" margarine or the pie crust won't work.

1 cup Flour blend (page 41)
¾ cup tapioca flour
½ cup sweet rice flour
1 tablespoon sugar
1 teaspoon xanthan gum
1 teaspoon guar gum
1 teaspoon herbes de Provence
   or dried thyme leaves

½ teaspoon salt
½ cup shortening*
2 tablespoons butter/buttery spread (non-diet)
¼ cup milk (cow, rice, soy)
Egg wash (optional)
Filling for 6 people (use beef stew, chicken
   soup, or vegetable stew thickened to taste)
Non-hydrogenated shortenings, made by Spectrum® or Smart Balance®, are available at health food stores.

1. Preheat oven to 375°F. Fill greased 13 x 9-inch casserole dish with filling of choice such as vegetable stew, beef stew, or chicken soup (thickened to desired consistency). Put casserole dish in oven to start baking.

2. Place dry ingredients, shortening, and butter in food processor. Mix well. Add milk and blend until dough forms ball.

3. Flatten dough to 1-inch disk, wrap tightly, and chill 1 hour so liquids are well distributed. (If time is short, proceed directly to rolling out the dough.)

4. If dough has been chilled, massage dough between hands until warm and pliable, making crust easier to handle. Roll half of dough to rectangle between two pieces of heavy-duty plastic wrap dusted with rice flour. Use damp paper towel between countertop and plastic wrap to anchor plastic wrap. Keep remaining half wrapped tightly to avoid drying out if you don't need it. Be sure to move rolling pin from center of dough to outer edge, moving around in clockwise fashion to assure uniform thickness.

5. Remove casserole from oven. Remove top plastic wrap and invert crust onto palm of other hand. Remove remaining plastic wrap and center crust over filling being careful not to touch hot filling or hot casserole dish. Brush with beaten egg. Return casserole to oven and bake for 25 to 30 minutes or until crust is nicely browned. Serves 6.

Based on using beef stew:
Calories 660; Fat 27g; Protein 26g; Carbohydrates 85g; Sodium 680mg; Cholesterol 71mg; Fiber <1g

⊰• Chili Cornbread Casserole •⊱

You can make the chili filling ahead of time and freeze it. Then, when you're pressed for time and need a quick meal, defrost the chili in the microwave while you mix up the cornbread crust. Gluten-free brands of cornmeal include Albers, Lamb's, Kinnikinnick, and Shiloh Farms.

Chili Filling	Cornbread Crust
1 pound ground round	⅔ cup Flour blend (page 41)
1 cup finely chopped onions	½ cup yellow gluten-free cornmeal
1 can (15 ounces) pinto or kidney beans	2 tablespoons sugar
1 can (15 ounces) canned tomatoes	1 teaspoon baking powder
2 teaspoons chili powder	½ teaspoon baking soda
½ teaspoon ground cumin	½ teaspoon salt
½ teaspoon ground coriander	½ teaspoon xanthan gum
1 teaspoon salt	1 large egg
Water (if too thick)	⅔ cup buttermilk or 1 tablespoon cider vinegar and enough non-dairy milk to equal ⅔ cup
	2 tablespoons canola oil

Chili Filling

1. In large Dutch oven or skillet, combine ground round and chopped onion. Cook over medium heat until meat and onion are gently browned. Add remaining ingredients, cover, and simmer on low 2 hours. Or, cook in slow cooker 4 to 6 hours.

2. Preheat oven to 375ºF. Grease 9 x 13-inch pan or 10-inch cast-iron skillet. Pour in chili. Set aside. (If chili is not hot, put in oven to heat up while making corn bread.)

Cornbread Crust

1. In medium bowl, combine all ingredients. Blend with electric mixer until smooth.

2. Pour cornbread batter over chili filling, spreading to edges of pan.

3. Bake 20 to 25 minutes or until top is firm and lightly browned. Serve warm. Serves 6.

Calories 650; Fat 20g; Protein 36g; Carbohydrates 85g; Sodium 928mg; Cholesterol 83mg; Fiber 20g

✑ Corn Bread & Sausage Stuffing ✑

Use this easy recipe whenever you want stuffing. Of course, most of us have personal preferences about stuffing so you may need to alter the seasoning accordingly. If you use my corn bread recipe on page 73, you'll need to make two batches.

12 to 14 cups cubed gluten-free corn bread
½ pound gluten-free sausage
1 medium onion, finely chopped
3 stalks celery, finely chopped
3 teaspoons ground sage

1 teaspoon celery seed
1 teaspoon dried oregano
½ teaspoon salt
½ teaspoon white pepper
2 cups gluten-free chicken broth

Brown sausage, onion, and celery in heavy skillet over medium heat. Drain well. Combine corn bread with remaining ingredients, stirring well. Turn into greased 9 x 13-inch dish. Bake 30 to 40 minutes at 350°F until browned—or loosely stuff turkey with corn bread mixture and bake remainder in 11 x 7-inch greased casserole. Makes about 8 to 10 cups. Serves 16 (½ cup each).

Calories 225; Fat 7g; Protein 7g; Carbohydrates 34g; Sodium 684mg; Cholesterol 11mg; Fiber 2g

✑ Bread Stuffing ✑

This is the traditional stuffing for turkey, chicken, or pork chops. Vary the spices to suit your taste.

2 loaves gluten-free bread, cubed
1 large finely chopped onion
4 stalks finely chopped celery
1 teaspoon canola oil
4 teaspoons dried sage
2 teaspoons poultry seasoning

2 teaspoons celery salt
2 teaspoons celery seed
1 teaspoon dried parsley
½ teaspoon white pepper
4 cups gluten-free chicken broth

1. Sauté onion and celery in oil until just tender and slightly translucent. Combine all remaining ingredients with cubed bread and toss lightly until just moistened.

2. Loosely stuff turkey with bread mixture—or bake in greased casserole dish at 350°F for 30 to 40 minutes or until nicely browned. Makes about 10 to 12 cups. Serves 20 (½ cup each).

Calories 175; Fat 1g; Protein 6g; Carbohydrates 34g; Sodium 246mg; Cholesterol 0mg; Fiber 1g

☙• Swiss Steak •❧

This was an old stand-by when my son was growing up. I made it in an old electric skillet and it always pleased everybody. Beau Monde seasoning is made by Spice Islands.

1 pound round steak, 1-inch thick
1 tablespoon olive oil
¼ cup chopped onions
1 can (16 ounces) diced tomatoes

1 tablespoon diced green pepper
1 teaspoon Beau Monde seasoning
¼ teaspoon dried basil
¼ teaspoon salt

Brown steaks on both sides in olive oil over medium heat. Add remaining ingredients, bring to boil, and then reduce heat to low. Cover and simmer for 30 minutes. Serves 4 (¼ pound each).

Calories 275; Fat 16g; Protein 26g; Carbohydrates 5g; Sodium 639mg; Cholesterol 68mg; Fiber 1g

☙• Tuna Noodle Casserole •❧

You don't have to give up this favorite family casserole. Jazz it up with water chestnuts, chopped pimiento, topped with crushed potato chips, or Parmesan cheese for added flavor. Penne pasta holds its shape well after cooking, but use any pasta you like.

4 cups cooked gluten-free pasta*
1 can (6 ounces) low-salt tuna in water,
  drained
1 can (18 ounces) Cream of Mushroom
  soup (Progresso is gluten-free)
Gluten-free brands are Pastariso, DeBole's, Ener-G, Annie's, and Tinkyada, available at your local health food store. Bean pasta is at www.heartlandsfinest.com. Dr. Schar pasta is available at www.glutensolutions.com and www.glutenfreepantry.com

½ cup green peas
1 tablespoon instant minced onion
¼ teaspoon celery salt
½ teaspoon fresh dill weed or ¼
  teaspoon dried
⅛ teaspoon white pepper
Sprinkle of paprika (optional)

1. Preheat oven to 350°F. Grease 9 x 9-inch casserole dish.

2. In large bowl, thoroughly combine tuna, soup, peas, onions, celery salt, dill, and pepper. Gently stir in cooked pasta. Mixture may be "soupy." Transfer to prepared pan. Sprinkle with paprika.

3. Bake 15 to 20 minutes or until hot. Serves 4 (1 cup each).

Calories 390; Fat 12g; Protein 20g; Carbohydrates 51g; Sodium 999mg; Cholesterol 19mg; Fiber 3g

∞• Mexican Casserole •∞

This is a great make-ahead casserole just right for weeknights, but also makes a great dish for entertaining friends. You may use non-dairy cheeses made from soy or rice, if you wish.

1 cup gluten-free chicken broth
1 cup Rotel® Mexican tomatoes
1 medium onion, finely diced
1 can (4 ounces) diced green chiles
½ teaspoon dried oregano
¼ teaspoon ground cumin
¼ teaspoon ground sage
¼ teaspoon chili powder

¼ teaspoon garlic powder
½ teaspoon salt
2 cups cooked chicken, cubed
1 cup grated cheddar cheese
1 cup grated Monterey Jack cheese
2 cups corn tortilla chips
2 tablespoons chopped cilantro

1. Preheat oven to 350ºF. Mix chicken broth, tomatoes, onions, green chiles, spices, and salt together in bowl to form sauce. Set aside.

2. Grease 10 x 14-inch casserole dish. Layer half of the chicken, then half of the sauce, cheese, and corn tortilla chips. Repeat layers, ending with cheese.

3. Bake 35 to 40 minutes or until casserole is bubbly. To serve, garnish with chopped cilantro. Serves 6.

Calories 330; Fat 21g; Protein 24g; Carbohydrates 12g; Sodium 811mg; Cholesterol 80mg; Fiber 2g

ᘓ• White Sauce •ᘔ

Sometimes called Bechamel Sauce, this basic sauce is useful in many ways. And, you can vary the seasonings to achieve the taste you want.

1 cup milk (cow, rice, soy—¼ cup reserved)
1 cup gluten-free chicken broth (low sodium)
1 small onion, quartered (with a whole clove stuck in it)

2 tablespoons butter or olive oil
1 small bay leaf
3 tablespoons cornstarch

1. Combine all ingredients (except cornstarch) in heavy saucepan. Heat just to a simmer; then remove from heat and let stand 5 minutes. Remove onion, clove, and bay leaf.

2. Stir cornstarch into reserved ¼ cup milk to form paste. Stir paste into milk and heat over medium heat, whisking constantly, until mixture boils. Reduce heat to low and continue to cook, whisking constantly, another minute. Makes 2 cups. Serves 4 (½ cup each).
Calories 120; Fat 7g; Protein 4g; Carbohydrates 10g; Sodium 75mg; Cholesterol 20mg; Fiber <1g

ᘓ• Onion Soup Mix •ᘔ

Use this handy mix in place of the commercial variety, in the same amount. Gluten-free bouillons include Albertson's, Ener-G, Herb Ox, and Hy-Vee.

½ cup dried minced onions
1 tablespoon sweet rice flour
1 teaspoon onion salt
½ teaspoon gluten-free bouillon powder

¼ teaspoon garlic powder
¼ teaspoon sugar
¼ teaspoon celery seed
¼ teaspoon apple pectin powder

Combine ingredients in screw-top jar. Store in dark, dry place. Use in same proportions as commercial onion soup mix. Double or triple recipe, if needed. Makes about ⅓ cup.
Per tablespoon:
Calories 25; Fat 0g; Protein 1g; Carbohydrates 6g; Sodium 334mg; Cholesterol 0mg; Fiber <1g

❧• Cream of Mushroom Soup •❧

Many casseroles require this soup as a base. If you can't find Progresso® mushroom soup or want to make your own, use this versatile recipe to make the equivalent of one can of soup, reconstituted.

1 can (7 ounces) sliced mushrooms*
⅓ cup butter/buttery spread, divided
1 cup milk (cow, rice, or soy)
½ cup dry milk powder (cow, rice, soy-not Carnation)
1 tablespoon dried minced onions
½ teaspoon guar gum
Fresh mushrooms turn dark

½ teaspoon celery salt
½ teaspoon salt
½ teaspoon dry mustard**
¼ teaspoon garlic powder
⅛ teaspoon white pepper
2 tablespoons sweet rice flour
¼ cup milk
**Grind mustard seeds with coffee grinder or use Durkee or McCormick.*

1. In medium saucepan, sauté drained mushrooms in 1 tablespoon of butter over medium heat. Remove from heat; add milk and remaining butter. Stir together dry milk and next 7 ingredients (onion through pepper) and add to pan.

2. Stir sweet rice flour into ¼ cup milk to form paste. Whisk mixture into pan, return to medium heat, and continue whisking until mixture thickens. Remove from heat. Cool. Makes 2 cups. Serves 4 (½ cup each).
Calories 240; Fat 17g; Protein 7g; Carbohydrates 16g; Sodium 775mg; Cholesterol 49mg; Fiber 1g

Cream of Chicken Soup: Add 2 tablespoons chicken bouillon granules to dry ingredients. (Ener-G makes a gluten-free version) and ¼ cup finely chopped chicken. Omit celery salt and salt.
Calories 265; Fat 19g; Protein 10g; Carbohydrates 16g; Sodium 860mg; Cholesterol 57mg; Fiber 1g

Notes

❧ Appendices ❧
Associations & Resources

The following is a partial list of resources for gluten-free diets. This list is not intended as an endorsement of these companies and their phone numbers, addresses, and other contact information may change over time.

Allergy & Asthma Network, Mothers Of Asthmatics, Inc. 3554 Chain Ridge Road, Suite 200 Fairfax, VA 22030-2709 800.878.4403 (help line); 703.385.4403	**American Academy of Allergy, Asthma & Immunology** 611 E. Wells Street Milwaukee, WI 53202 800.822-2762 (help line); 414. 272.6071
American Celiac Disease Alliance 2504 Duxbury Place Alexandria, VA 22308 703.622.3331 www.americanceliac.org	**American Diabetes, Inc.** 1660 Duke Street Alexandria, VA 22314 800.DIABETES or 800.232.3472 www.diabetes.org
American Dietetic Association 120 S. Riverside Plaza, Suite 2000 Chicago, Ill., 60606 312.899.0040 www.eatright.org	**Asthma/Allergy Foundation of America** 1125 15th Street, N.W., Suite 502 Washington, D.C. 20005 800.7ASTHMA (help line) 202.466.7643 fax www.aafa.org
Autism Society of America 7910 Woodmont Ave., Suite 300 Bethesda, MD 20814-3015 800.3Autism, ext. 150 or 301.657.0881; 303.657.0869 fax	**Autism Network-Diet. Intervention (ANDI)** PO Box 335 Pennington, NJ 05834 www.autismndi.com
Autism Resource Network 904 Main Street Hopkins, MN 55343 952.988.0088; 952.988.0099 fax www.autismshop.com	**Celiac Center (Harvard-Beth Israel)** 330 Brookline Avenue Boston, MA 02215 617.667.7000 www.bidmc.harvard.edu/celiaccenter
Celiac Disease Center, Columbia University New York Presbyterian Hospital 161 Fort Washington Avenue New York, NY 10032 212.305.5590 www.celiacdiseasecenter.columbia.edu	**Celiac Disease Clinic, Mayo Clinic** **Celiac Disease Research Program** 200 First St. S.W. Rochester, MN 55905 507.284.2511 www.mayoclinic.org

Associations & Resources
(continued)

Celiac Disease Foundation 13251 Ventura Blvd., Suite 1 Studio City, CA 91604-1838 818.990.2354; 818.990.2379 fax http://www.celiac.org/cdf	**Celiac Disease Center** University of Chicago 5839 S. Maryland Ave. MC 4065 Chicago, IL 60637-1470 773 702 7593; 773 702 0666 fax www.celiacdisease.net
Celiac Sprue Association/USA PO Box 31700 Omaha, NE 68131-0700 402.558.0600; 402.558.1347 fax www.csaceliacs.org	**Center for Celiac Research** University of Maryland 20 Penn Street, Room S303B Baltimore, MD 21201 www.celiaccenter.org
Feingold Association of U.S. PO Box 6550 Alexandria, VA 22306 800.321.3287 www.feingold.org	**Fine, MD., Dr. Kenneth** Intestinal Health Institute (web site about celiac disease and other forms of gluten sensitivity) www.enterolab.com www.finerhealth.com
Food Allergy/Anaphylaxis Network (FAAN) 11781 Lee Jackson Hwy., Suite 160 Fairfax, VA 22033-3309 800.929.4040 or 703.691.3179 http://www.foodallergy.org http:// www.fankids.org (for kids)	*Gluten-Free Living* **Magazine** 560 Warburton Avenue Hastings-on-Hudson, NY 10706 914.7415.420 www.glutenfreeliving.com
Gluten Intolerance Group of No. Amer. 15110 10th Avenue SW, Suite A Seattle, WA 98166-1820 206.246.6652; 206.246.6531 fax www.gluten.net; gig@gluten.net	*Living Without* **Magazine** PO Box 2126 Northbrook, IL 60065 847.480.8810; 847.480.8810 fax www.livingwithout.com
Nat'l Attention Deficit Disorder Assoc. 1788 Second Street, Suite 200 Highland Park, IL 60035 847.432.2332 www.add.org	**Nat'l Foundation for Celiac Awareness** 224 South Maple Street Ambler, PA 19002 215.325.306;| 215.283.0859 fax www.CeliacCentral.org

Associations & Resources
(continued)

Nat'l Jewish Medical & Research Center	National Sorghum Producers
1400 Jackson Street	PO Box 5309
Denver, CO 80206	Lubbock, TX 79408
800.222.5864 (lung line) 303.388.4461	806 749 3478
www.njc.org	www.sorghumgrowers.com
(info on allergies, asthma, lung disease)	(info on table or white sorghum)

Mail Order & On-Line Sources
For Gluten-Free Ingredients & Products

This list is not an endorsement of any company. Names, addresses, phones, fax numbers, and e-mail addresses of these companies may change—as well as their product lines.

Authentic Foods 1850 W. 169th Street, Suite B Gardena, CA 90247 800.806.4737; 310.366.7612 fax www.authenticfoods.com (flours, ingredients, mixes)	**Better Batter** ~~10835 Lawrence 1217~~ ~~Mt. Vernon, MO 65712~~ ~~417.466.DIET (3438)~~ ~~www.betterbatter.com~~ ~~(foods free of gluten and soy)~~
Bob's Red Mill Natural Foods 13521 SE Pheasant Court Milwaukie, OR 97222 800.349.2173; 503.653.1339 fax www.bobsredmill.com (flours, grains, mixes)	**Bob & Ruth's Travel Club** 22 Breton Hill Rd. Suite 1B Pikesville, MD 21208 410.486.0292 bobolevy@juno.com (gluten-free newsletter & travel club)
Breads from Anna 877.354.3886 www.glutenevolutions.com (mixes)	**Cream Hill Estates** 9633 rue Clement Lasalle, Quebec H8R 4B4 866-727-3628 www.creamhillestates.com (gluten-free oats)
Dowd & Rogers, Inc. 1641 49th St. Sacramento, CA 95819 916.451.6480; 916.736.2349 fax www.dowdandrogers.com (chestnut flour mixes)	**Dietary Specialties** 10 Leslie Court Whippany, NJ 07981 888.640.2800 www.dietspec.com (foods, ingredients)
Edward & Sons, Inc. P.O. Box 1326 Carpinteria, CA 93014 805.684.8500; 805.684.8220 fax www.edwardandsons.com (rice crackers; gluten free products)	**Ener-G Foods, Inc.** 5960 First Ave. South Seattle, WA 98124 800.331.5222; 206.764.3398 fax www.ener-g.com (flours, ingredients, mixes)

Mail Order & On-Line Sources
for Gluten-Free Ingredients & Products (continued)

Enjoy Life Foods 1601 Natchez Avenue Chicago, IL 60707-4023 888.50.ENJOY; 773.889.5090 fax www.enjoylifefoods.com (cookies, bars, bagels)	**Gifts of Nature** 810 7th Street E #17 Polson, MT 59860 888.275.0003 www.giftsofnature.net (flours, mixes, gluten-free oats)
Glutenfreeda P.O. Box 1364 Glenwood Springs, CO 81602-1364 www.glutenfreeda.com (online cooking magazine; frozen cookie dough)	**Gluten-Free Oats** 578 Lane 9 Powell WY 82435 307.754.2058; 307.754.0924 (fax) www.glutenfreeoats.com pure, gluten-free oats
Gluten-Free Pantry (dba Glutino) PO Box 840 Glastonbury, CT 06033 800.291.8386 (orders); 860.633.6853 fax http://www.glutenfree.com (mixes, ingredients, appliances)	**Gluten Free Mall** www.glutenfreemall.com (many vendors offering flours, ingredients, mixes, food, bakery items, books, etc.)
Gluten-Free Market 1714 McHenry Road Buffalo Grove, IL 60089 847.419.9610; 847.419-9615 fax www.glutenfreemarket.com (foods, ingredients, books)	**Gluten Solutions, Inc.** 3810 Riviera Drive, Suite 1 San Diego, CA 92109 888 845-8836; 810.454.8277 fax www.glutensolutions.com (mixes, ingredients, books, food)
Gluten-Free Trading Co., LLC 3116 S Chase Avenue Milwaukee WI 53207 USA 888-993-9933; 414-747-8747 fax http://www.food4celiacs.com (flours, ingredients, mixes, foods)	**Glutino.com (DEROMA)** 3750 Francis Hughes, Laval, Quebec Canada H7L-5A9 800.363.DIET; 450.629.4781 fax www.glutino.com (mixes, ingredients, baked items)
Goodday Health 514A North Western Ave. Lake Forest, IL 60045 877.395.2527; 847.615.1209 fax gooddayglutenfree@msn.com (gluten-free items, all major vendors)	**Heartland Ingredients** (Heartland's Finest) P.O. Box 313 Ubly, MI., 48475 888 658-8909; 989-658-8949 fax www.heartlandsfinest.com (bean pasta and flour)

Mail Order & On-Line Sources
for Gluten-Free Ingredients & Products (continued)

JatFoods, Inc. 5953 Dunegal Ct. Agoura Hills, CA 91301 818.706.1001; 818.991.0865 www.jatfoods.com (Dynemo nutritional energy bars)	**King Arthur Flour** PO Box 876 Norwich, VT 05055-0876 800.827.6836; 800.343-3002 fax www.bakerscatalogue.com (flours, xanthan gum, mixes)
Kinnikinnick Foods 10940-120 Street Edmonton, AB,Canada, T5H 3P7 877.503.4466; 780.421.0456 www.kinnikinnick.com (flours, foods, ingredients)	**Mary's Gone Crackers** P.O. Box 1688 Orinda, CA 94563 *888.258.1250; 925-258-1201 fax* www.marysgonecrackers.com whole grain crackers
Miss Roben's (Allergy Grocer) 91 Western Maryland Pkwy. Suite 1 Hagerstown, MD 21740 800.891.0083; 301.665.9584 fax www.missroben.com (baking mixes, ingredients)	**Montina (Amazing Grains)** 405 West Main Ronan, MT 59864 877.278.6585; 406.676.0677 fax www.montina.com (Indian rice grass flour, products)
Mrs. Leeper's 1000 Italian Way Excelsior Springs, MO 816. 502.6000; 816.502.6722 fax www.mrsleeperspasta.com (gluten-free pasta)	**Namaste Foods** P.O. Box 3133 Coeur d'Alene, ID 83816 866.258.9493; 208.676.9632 www.namastefoods.com (mixes)
Natural Feast Pies & Products 150 Main Street, Suite 11 Richmond, ME 04357 866.628.6346; 207.737.2237 fax www.naturalfeast.com (gluten-free pies)	**Nature's Hilights, Inc.** P.O. Box 3526 Chico, CA 95927 800-313-6454; 530-342-3130 www.natures-hilights.com (pizza crusts, snacks, brownies)
NuWorld Amaranth (NuWorldFoods) PO Box 2202 Naperville, IL 60567 630-369-6819; 630-369-6851 fax www.nuworldfoods.com (amaranth flour, foods, mixes)	**Only Oats (Farm Pure Foods)** 316-1st Avenue East Regina, Saskatchewan, S4N 5H2 Canada 866.461.FOOD (3663); 306.757.1218 fax www.onlyoats.com (gluten-free oats and mixes)

Mail Order & On-Line Sources
for Gluten-Free Ingredients & Products (continued)

Pamela's Products 200 Clara Avenue Ukiah, CA 95482 707-462-6605; 707-462-6642 fax www.pamelasproducts.com (cookies, mixes at gluten-free vendors)	**Premium Gold Packaging, Inc.** 1321 12th Ave. NE Denhoff, ND 58430 701.884.2553 pgp@westriv.com (fine ground flax meal)
Ruby Range 1231 Willow Lane Estes Park, CO 80517 970.577.0888; 970.577.9547 fax www.therubyrange.com (mesquite & teff mixes)	**Sylvan Border Farm** P.O. Box 277 Willits, CA 95490-0277 800.297.5399; 707.459.1834 fax www.sylvanborderfarm.com (mixes, ingredients)
Twin Valley Mills, LLC R.R. 1, Box 45 Ruskin, NE 68974 402.279.3965 www.twinvalleymills.com (sorghum flour)	**Vance's Foods** P.O. Box 255734 Sacramento, California 95865 800.497.4834; 800-497-4329 fax www.vancesfoods.com (gluten-free milk powder and liquid)

Meet Carol Fenster, Ph.D.

What began as a solution to her own wheat intolerance grew into an internationally-recognized corporation, serving people with food allergies, celiac disease, and autism. Today, Carol has authored eight cookbooks and is actively involved and recognized as a leader in the area of food sensitivities.

• She appeared on the Health Network, PBS, and is a guest speaker at the American Dietetic Association, Gluten Intolerance Group, Natural Products Expo, Gluten-Free Culinary Summit, Disney, Whole Grains Council, FoodEX-Tokyo.

• She develops gluten-free mixes for Bob's Red Mill Natural Foods and consults with food manufacturers, offers cooking classes, and advises entrepreneurs.

• She conducts seminars on the use of sorghum in gluten-free diets in Japan with the U.S. Grains Council and in Italy with the Institute of Biophysics and Genetics.

• Articles, recipes, and reviews of her books appear in *Reader's Digest, Cooking Smart, Natural Health, Woman's World, Taste for Life, Vegetarian Times, Better Nutrition, Energy Times, Gluten-Free Living, Living Without, Today's Dietitian*, and newsletters by Food Allergy and Anaphylaxis Network (FAAN), Gluten Intolerance Group, and Celiac Disease Foundation. She recently launched a weekly online menu planning service at www.gfreecuisine.com. She is a member of the American Celiac Disease Alliance and International Association of Culinary Professionals.

• She holds an undergraduate degree in Home Economics from the University of Nebraska and a doctorate in Organizational Sociology from the University of Denver, where she was also a faculty member. To contact her:

Savory Palate, Inc.
8174 South Holly Street, #404
Centennial, CO 80122-4004
800.741.5418   303.741.5408   303.741-0339 fax
http//www.savorypalate.com   carol@savorypalate.com

Subscribe to Carol's free newsletter, "Carol's Culinary Cues" at www.glutenfree101.com
and
Subscribe to her weekly gluten-free online menu planning service at www.gfreecuisine.com

INDEX

Gluten Solutions, 35, 167, 171, 172, 178, 187
Gluten-Free Living magazine, i, vi, x 7, 31, 184
Gluten-Free Mall, 187
Gluten-Free Market, 187
Gluten-Free Oats, 6, 17, 107, 144-145, 156, 186
Gluten-Free Pantry, 11, 167, 171-172, 178, 187
Gluten-Free Trading Co, 187
Glutino, 3, 35, 187
Goodday Health, 187
Granola, 34, 107
Gravy, 163
Guar gum, 24, 43, 457

-H-
Ham & Scalloped Potatoes, 164
Hamburger Buns, 76
Heartland's Finest, 3, 167, 171-172, 178, 187
Hemp seed, 54
Herb Buns, 76
Hicks, John, i
High-Fiber Bread, 65
Hoggan, Ron, 7
HolGrain, 3
Hot Dog Buns, 76
Hummus, 3
Hydrolyzed vegetable protein, 30

-I-
Ice cream, 3
IgE, 5, 8
Imitation vanilla, 31
Indian rice grass, 4, 16, 29, 45, 53, 61, 174, 188

Individuals with Disabilities Ed Act (IDEA), 11
Italy, 35

-J-
Jat Foods, 187

-K-
King Arthur Flour, 188
Kinnikinnick Foods, 3, 73, 162, 165, 166, 187, 188
Korn, Danna, 7
Kudzu, 24
Kupper, Cynthia, i

-L-
Labels, x, 26-32
Lemon Bars, 149
Lemon Cake, 117
Lemon Sauce, 128
Lemon Cranberry Muffins, 88
Lemon Poppy Seed Coffee Cake, 100
Lemon Poppy Seed Muffins, 89
Lewis, Lisa, 7
Libonati, Cleo, *7*
Living Without magazine, 35-36, 184
Lotus root starch, 44
Lundberg, 3

-M-
Macaroni & Cheese, 167
Mail-Order, On-Line Sources, 186
Main Dishes, 3, 159-182
Malted milk, 30
Mary's Gone Crackers, 3, 33, 188
Meat Loaf, 168
Mexican Casserole, 179
Mexican Wedding Cakes, 134